# Chains of the Spirit

## A Manual for Liberation

### Tim Timmons

Canon Press

Washington, D. C.

Copyright 1973 Canon Press, Washington, D. C.

ISBN #0913686 07-7

These words come from the Lord Jesus Christ and the ancient biblical prophet Isaiah. Accompanying the striking cover design by Joe DeValasco, they picture Satan who chains the spirits of men.

*And He [Jesus] said to them, "I was*
*watching Satan fall from heaven*
*like lightning." (Luke 10:18, brackets added)*

*"How you have fallen from heaven,*
*O star of the morning, son of the dawn!*
*You have been cut down to the earth,*
*You who have weakened the nations!*
*"But you said in your heart,*
*'I will ascend to heaven;*
*I will raise my throne above the stars of God,*
*And I will sit on the mount of assembly*
*In the recesses of the north.*
*'I will ascend above the heights of the clouds;*
*I will make myself like the Most High . . .'*
*"But you have been cast out of your tomb*
*Like a rejected branch,*
*Clothed with the slain who are pierced with a sword . . ."*
*(Isaiah 14:12-14, 19a)*

# CONTENTS

# PREFACE

If someone had asked me seven years ago, "Do you believe in the power or existence of the spirit world?" I would have hesitated, not knowing what to answer. Today, I give an emphatic "yes."

Why? Because I have seen it! As director of a Christian organization on a college campus I noticed that some students I met had severe problems—problems that were out of my realm. So I began studying biblical principles dealing with the spirit world's forces and how to get free from their grip. Though many amulets and incantations have been used throughout the centuries to resist evil spirits, the biblical perspective seemed to make the most sense. With this to guide me, I eventually felt prepared to deal with the problems that had stumped me before.

Having a reputation as a Christian speaker on the campus, I was called one evening by a student government leader. "Tim, I've got to talk to you tonight!" he blurted out in panic. I met him at the student center minutes later. He fidgeted, pouring out an incredible story. He had just come from a seance where he had encountered the spirit world face to face. He was obsessed by the voices from the weird meeting—and was he scared! When he finished his tale, so was I! Having seen and experienced the spiritual forces of darkness, he realized that what I had been speaking about was also true; that night he came to know the true Liberator —the Lord Jesus Christ.

The next day a girl called. Her roommate was a white witch who had read her future from tarot cards. She had told her a young man would come into her life and bring good fortune. A few evenings after this prediction, a fiery

1

light had appeared to her communicating that it had come to fulfill the prophecy. Screaming, she ran from the room in terror, afraid to tell anyone what had happened. The next night the fire had returned again. Now she was calling me for help! She, too, came to know Jesus Christ in a personal way and found freedom by applying the biblical principles of liberation.

During that week six people came to me desperately seeking help. All were oppressed or controlled by forces of the spirit world; all were liberated by applying biblical principles. One was even released from homosexuality!

Since then, God has given me hundreds of opportunities to help people bound by the CHAINS OF THE SPIRIT. Seeing their freedom and joy in release, I have been encouraged to share these biblical principles in this Manual for Liberation.

# INTRODUCTION

Life is full of struggles! Everyone is confronted with the social struggles of our time—racial prejudice, economic injustices, bizarre killings, senseless crime, the ecological crisis, corruption in business and government, the atrocities of war. . . . A few attack these problems with everything they can muster. But it doesn't take long to discover that even the strongest efforts of the few are but a drop in the bucket, in light of the overwhelming multiplication of factors. Their efforts are futile, placing Band-Aids on the hemorrhages of a rupturing society. The rest passively ignore the problems—at least until they strike close to home.

Even more universal is the confrontation with personal struggles: the quest for self-identity and purpose in life, the need to love and be loved, to be respected, to meaningfully express oneself, and the need for security and sense of accomplishment. Most people diligently search for answers to these personal struggles or seek an escape from facing responsibilities connected with them. The search for answers is often as productive as grasping at a smoke ring, while escape leads to experimentation in such areas as alcohol, drugs, occultism, and ultimately suicide.

Yet behind these surface struggles is the real battle of life —the spiritual war. Jesus frequently taught about the demonic activity of the spirit world. He referred to demons and the leader of demons, Satan. The Apostle Paul expressed clearly what is the real battle when he wrote, "For our struggle is not against flesh and blood, but against the rulers, against the powers, against the world-forces of this darkness, against the spiritual forces of wickedness in the heavenly places" (Ephesians 6:12).

Today Christians and non-Christians alike, overlooking these warnings, have shifted toward an unusual fascination with the supernatural.

People are drawn to various supernatural acts, from predictions of the future to miraculous physical healings. Certainly God can do any and all of these, but so can the great counterfeiter, Satan, who disguises himself as an "angel of light" (II Corinthians 11:14). Many of these phenomena are part of a master scheme to lure people into spiritual captivity. It is a war for the lives of men!

In warfare three very basic principles lead to sure defeat when violated. The first is the realization that a war is going on. The soldier who sits in the barracks refusing to believe in the reality of war, while his building is being shelled, is in big trouble! The second principle is knowing the enemy's strategies and methods. The great militarists have been faithful students of their enemies. Neglect in this area contributes to sure defeat. The third principle is knowing how to fight. A man can be certain that he is in a battle and know all there is to know about his enemy, but if he does not know how to fight, he is in for destruction.

In spiritual warfare many believers in Christ, who already have the promise of victory over the enemy, are experiencing daily defeats. Most of these defeats result from ignorance of one of the three basic principles of warfare. First, they ignore the reality of spiritual war. A tragic number of believers are under the impression that spiritual warfare is only the battle of their old sinful nature against their new nature in Christ. These believers have one thing in common—they are defeated in their daily experience by demonic activity. Second, they do not know Satan's strategies and methods. Although much Scripture tells about the person and work of Satan, believers are extremely ignorant about him. Satan's devices are not always filthy or frightening in appearance, as many imagine. Third, believers are ignorant of their role in spiritual warfare against the devices of their enemy. The question that haunts the believer is "How do I fight the spiritual war?" Various answers are given, ranging from "be Spirit-filled" to "shut your eyes and it will go away" to "cast it out." These different answers come from either overemphasizing theological theory without reality, or overemphasizing experience without understanding the Word.

Two statements of caution are necessary to approaching this explosive subject of Satan and his demons. Both are taken from Christ's words of caution. At the beginning of Luke 10 the Lord appointed seventy men to go and minister ahead of him in many cities. They returned rejoicing over their trip, especially excited about the power they had in Christ's name over the demons. Here is their conversation with the Lord:

> And the seventy returned with joy, saying, "Lord, even the demons are subject to us in Your name."
>
> And He said to them, "I was watching Satan fall from heaven like lightning.
>
> "Behold, I have given you authority to tread upon serpents and scorpions, and over all the power of the enemy, and nothing shall injure you." (Luke 10:17-19)
>
> Jesus brought the situation into perspective by saying,
>
> "Nevertheless do not rejoice in this, that the spirits are subject to you, but rejoice that your names are recorded in heaven." (Luke 10:20)

The two cautions are: (1) *Be careful of becoming a "demon inspector."* It is very easy to take the list of symptoms of demonic influence, diagnosing some of your friends and all of your enemies. The demon inspector is continually looking over his shoulder for another demon in times of adversity, forgetting that many problems and weird happenings occur that are not caused by Satan and his demons. (2) *Be careful of being demon-centered rather than Christ-centered.* The subject of demon activity is as exciting as prophecy—and this excitement spreads rapidly. But the believer must not make the subject of Satan and his devices more of his conversation than speaking of Christ and his salvation work.

CHAINS OF THE SPIRIT has four chapters: "Recognizing"—how to discover possible symptoms of demonic activity; "Reckoning"—how the believer acts in regard to his sin nature; "Renewing"—how the believer treats what the Bible calls the world; "Resisting"—how the believer combats Satan. The first chapter answers the question: How can I discern what is demonic activity? The last three chapters answer the question: How do I fight the spiritual war to the fullest? This book attempts to balance principles of the Word with practical experience. I trust that it will be a practical aid providing biblical principles for those fighting spiritual warfare.

# CHAPTER 1

# Recognizing

Recognizing Satan's activity in your life is vital to fighting the spiritual battle. When it comes to discerning whether a given problem is of the devil, there is a wide range of opinion—the spectrum runs from "it's all in your head" to "when in doubt, cast it out." Before beginning we need guidelines to help in our detection. The following three areas necessary for recognizing demonic activity will be discussed: (1) Satan's traps, (2) facets of his attack, and (3) testing the spirits.

## SATAN'S TRAPS

Satan is not stupid! He knows that the proverbial red-suited, two-horned, long-tailed, ugly-looking creature, with pitchfork in hand, lures few men into his trap. He is nevertheless successful with another approach that shows him to be evil—the upsurging Satanist movement throughout the world. More often Satan uses a disguise, concealing his real identity to present himself in a more favorable way. He disguises himself as an "angel of light" (II Corinthians 11:14), appearing to men as a messenger of that which is good and wholesome to imply that he is from God. This is the same way he approached Jesus in the wilderness. He did not appear to Jesus to offer him something intrinsically bad, but to offer him genuinely good things. Behind these good things was the snare—Satan was trying to lure Jesus into acting independently of the Father.

Satan is more than willing to give good things, but in order to obtain them you must do it his way. His way of independence always short-circuits dependence on God and his Word. He enjoys counterfeiting everything that God as to offer—all to trap unsuspecting people.

People everywhere are finding themselves victims of uncontrollable physical, emotional and spiritual problems without knowing their sources. The Bible warns of three major traps that Satan uses—the occult trap, the religious trap, and the sin trap. Every device that Satan has is used in one of these traps.

## THE OCCULT TRAP

"Interest in the occult, for decades the domain of tiny coteries, has suddenly emerged as a mass phenomenon in the United States. Increasing thousands of Americans are now active practitioners of witchcraft, spiritualism, magic, and even devil worship. Millions more are addicted to astrology, numerology, fortune-telling and tarot cards." [1] Most people view this mass phenomenon as intriguing and harmless, but there are some who are convinced that occult practices are not so harmless, but in fact extremely dangerous. Dr. Kurt E. Koch in *Christian Counselling and Occultism* recognizes the coincidence between psychic disturbance and occult participation. He points out that:

> (the) neurosis epidemic corresponds on the counseling level to the post-war flood of psychical disturbances, which in many observed instances stand in noteworthy frequency ratio to the increasing occult practices. 'Insecure' man seeks in every manner to escape the growing unknown about the fate of his dear ones, about the threatening future, about health, and about mere existence, and consequently takes recourse for help to occult manipulation. [2] (parentheses added)

Dr. William S. Reed, a U. S. psychiatrist, says, "Many mental and physical illnesses result, in fact, from demonic attacks." [3] Even within the occult camp there is concern over the serious effects people are experiencing from participation in the occult. The quarterly magazine, *Occult,* in its first edition of 1973, included an article entitled "Why I Started a Psychic Rescue Squad" that discusses severe problems caused directly by occult activity.

The Bible also convinces us that the occult is dangerous and warns of tampering with any part of it. The Lord makes it clear that he hates occult practices; in Deuteronomy 18:9-13 he lists various activities of the occult and says that he finds them detestable. He also says:

> . . . thou shalt not learn to do after the abominations of these nations. There shall not be found with thee any one . . . that useth divination (fortune-teller), or an observer of the times (soothsayer), or an enchanter (magician), or a witch (sorceress), or a charmer (hypnotist), or a consulter with familiar spirits (medium controlled by a spirit), or a wizard (clairvoyant or psychic), or a necromancer (medium who consults the dead). For all that do these things are an abomination unto the Lord. (Deuteronomy 18:9-13, KJV, parentheses added)

The word, occult, refers to things covered over, mysterious, concealed, or hidden. The occult goes beyond the human understanding and five senses. The following six important characteristics of the occult help us to discover the nature of its traps. (1) *In every occult practice there is contact with the spirit world.* The spirit world does not consist of spirits of the dead, but of angelic beings—both good and bad. The bad spirits that are linked with the occult are fallen angels who followed Lucifer's (Satan's) rebellion, remaining in subjection to him (Matthew 12:24). Satan uses his army of spirits, demons, to carry out his wicked strategy. An organized system within the ranks of demons (Ephesians 6:11-12) possibly involves the assignment of demons to specific individuals so that they can know these persons fully, including their weaknesses and strengths. This could explain the incredibly intimate knowledge a "spirit of a departed loved one" reveals in a seance. It is not the spirit of the dead person speaking, but a demon who knew the person well. Most find this extremely difficult to believe because it is so realistic. In occult activity there is always some connection with the demonic spirit world.

One girl, after hearing me speak on the occult, came to me declaring that she could prove me wrong on this point from her own experience. Deeply entangled in transcendental meditation, she was convinced that she was looking only into her own being. She was certain that she was not communicating with any spirits—especially evil ones. After a brief conversation with her, I learned of some additional occult practices she had tried. She was rather unimpressed with what I had said, since these occult activities had made such a difference in her life. That night I remember praying that somehow she would come to realize the danger that was threatening. Three or four days later she called with fear in her voice, wanting to talk some more as soon as possible. She could not wait to tell what had happened to her since our talk. Just two days later she had been going through her regular meditation when suddenly a spirit entered her room. Like a bright ball of fire, it spoke to her telling her to stay away from me because I was out to do her harm. Understandably, she was frightened by the experience, but when she woke up the next morning she felt that it was all her imagination and not real. The next night the same thing happened; this time the spirit asked to be her guide throughout the remainder of her life. This was too much to handle—now she wanted help. Later as we talked, it was evident when and where she had given over her will to the spirit world. After only a few hours of conversation, she realized how she could get free from this influence of the evil spirits. It was a beautiful change to see!

Another girl with a similar experience also denied that she had any contact with evil spirits. Later, after she had placed her faith in Christ as her personal Savior, she told of knowing all along that the Guru who had lived in her heart had been the center of her life.

(2) *All occult practices involve uncovering some hidden knowlege of the past or future.* Some actually give daily guidance. Ever since the beginning of time, man has had an unusual desire to know the hidden secrets of the universe. This aspect of the occult attracts people more than any other. In every level of society there are seances regularly held to speak to the dead and inquire about the future. Institutes and conferences are being set up all over the world to help men delve into the deeper resources of the mind. The purpose of these conferences is to give fuller knowledge of oneself and of the world. Many of these courses teach how to get help in daily life from supernatural sources. One such course is Mind Control. In this course there are certainly some good principles taught, but strange things happen toward the end of the institute. On the last day they teach how to have two "counselors," male and female, come upon you. They are called "symbols of divine intelligence"; in order to get them to reveal themselves you must be in a meditative state. When they come, they identify themselves by name, and are at your service for any kind of advice and counsel. They are nothing more than spirits! People who allow these counselors to come upon them are no more than sophisticated mediums seeking knowledge through the symbols of divine intelligence. The Lord warns against this as detestable and dangerous.

One dentist's counselors' names were "George" and "Agnes." He learned much from them that could have been known only through supernatural means. The main purpose for having these counselors is to "read cases." Through the aid of the counselors one can tell what problems another is having with as little information as name, age, and location. Then the one who reads the case can send "energy" to the person with problems. The problem many face is that these counselors begin to control various actions and ultimately their lives.

For years a young girl who had an unsatiable desire for knowledge of true spiritual life was harassed by various antics of the spirit world. Spirits appeared to her and told her she was a witch; at times she actually did weird things that made her think the spirits were right. In her last two years of college she went often to the campus theater where she saw incredible sights. One spirit that appeared to her frequently in the theater began to harass her; he made it clear that if she ever returned another time, it would be her last. Frustrated and fearful, she finally left the university and went home. Shortly after arriving home she heard of the Mind Control institute which was being offered in a nearby city. She attended with interest, and like the others, prepared to receive her counselors on the last day. She asked for two special counselors—Jesus and Sarah Bernhardt. To her amazement the counselors came to her—one claiming to be Jesus and the other Sarah. A few days later Sarah left to be replaced by another female counselor, a peasant woman. This spirit refused to give her name and said, "Just call me Mama. It's not time for you to know. You'll know who I am soon enough." Within twenty-four hours the girl heard of a woman who performed operations and healings. Immediately she had an unusual desire to go to meet her—she felt driven there! When she arrived at the woman's house, she experienced an overwhelming assurance that this was where she belonged. The 75-year-old peasant woman told the girl that she would also heal people and perform many wonderful things some day. From that time on the young girl assisted the peasant woman in over 200 operations. The girl felt she was no longer with the evil spirits, but the good spirits. This was actually just as much of a trap as when she had been harassed by evil spirits, for the peasant lady was a medium controlled by an evil spirit. The girl is now a believer in the Lord Jesus Christ and realizes how Satan tried to trap her.

Many are being deceived similarly and are being drawn into the occult trap to find deeper knowledge. The Lord tells us that deeper knowledge has been revealed in his Word, in order that "the man of God may be adequate, equipped for every good work" (II Timothy 3:17). The Bible further comments, "If they speak not according to this word, it is because there is no light in them" (Isaiah 8:20, KJV).

(3) *Most occult practices promise to give the experience of power.* This is closely related to the preceding characteristic of discovering hidden knowledge. If you have hidden knowledge about a person or an event, you can have some power over them. However, the experience of power normally involves much more than just prior or hidden knowledge. Usually the occult gives supernatural power to perform some normal task in an unusual way, or to perform some unusual feat beyond comprehension. This characteristic of the occult hooks people because of its spectacular nature.

A white witch can cast a good spell on a man who then immediately becomes successful; a black witch can cast a bad spell on a man who will become deathly ill for a few weeks. In many spiritist groups around the world, a quick but forceful act of power is used to build up belief in the one exercising the power. This is sometimes done by placing a hand or some type of instrument on a man's head while pronouncing an incantation. The person falls down immediately as if he were shot. The one struck down becomes a believer in the one exerting the power—and fast! This is no time for doubting!

Another spectacular demonstration of power is occult healing. Very popular, this is the source of power in healing ranging from primitive witch-doctors to many modern-day faith-healers. Most people who are lured into occult participation by the experience of power presuppose that all that is supernatural must be from God. This is an extremely dangerous concept! More will be discussed about this false belief in the following chapter.

(4) *All occult practices may be passed on to the third and fourth generations in a family.* Seeking the spirit world for knowledge or power sets God aside for another god. The Lord places a rough penalty upon this form of idolatry when he says:

> Thou shalt have no other gods before me . . . for I the Lord thy God am a jealous God, visiting the iniquity of the fathers upon the children unto the third and fourth generation. . . . (Exodus 20:3, 5, KJV)

I can give many illustrations of this, but one seems to be especially striking. Sherry was the victim of her grandmother's participation in the occult. Sherry's grandmother was a "harmless" medium who delighted in involving her family in her mysterious activities. By nineteen, Sherry had often experienced deep depression, contemplating suicide. Her self-image had been obliterated, her morals gone. She claimed she had no control over many of the things she did. To top it all off, she had been seeing a psychiatrist for ten years who treated her for what he called depersonalization. Since the age of nine Sherry had been plagued with a strange problem: at times, when looking into a mirror, she would slip into a non-existent state. Still conscious, she would black out, feeling as if she were not there. Naturally she would panic when this happened, because she could not see anything.

As she poured out her problems to me, I discerned that

there might be a much deeper problem in the area of demonic activity. The more I probed, the more I was certain that somehow she had given over her will to the spirit world and was now reaping the benefits. We were able to trace the beginning of her depersonalization problem to within two to three weeks of her first encounter with the ouija board—under the supervision of her grandmother. It was all in her diary! Convinced of the demonic origin of her problem, I proceeded to take Sherry through the steps to triumph over these evil forces. From that time on, Sherry has been a different girl! No more depersonalization, and no more deep depression. Today she is a beautiful, confident young lady. She is free from this particular trap that Satan had set for her through her own family!

(5) *All occult practices require a meditative, passive state before the spirit world can operate properly.* Unless a person submits and empties himself, the spirits cannot guide or take control. Jesus, replying to an attack from the Pharisees, described a man who was in a state very desirable for evil spirits to enter him. He said:

> Now when the unclean spirit goes out of a man, it passes through waterless places, seeking rest, and does not find it.
>
> Then it says, 'I will return to my house from which I came;' and when it comes, it finds it *unoccupied, swept, and put in order.*
>
> Then it goes, and takes along with it seven other spirits more wicked than itself, and they go in and live there; and the last state of that man becomes worse than the first. . . . (Matthew 12:43-45, italics added)

Three characteristics show how the state of the man encouraged the one evil spirit to bring seven friends along: "unoccupied, swept, and put in order." A more accurate translation might be: ". . . he finds it standing idle, having been swept and having been set in order." [4] The present action of the man is "standing idle." This is from the Greek word *scholazo,* which means "to be occupied with or concentrated on being passive, a state of being idle, or giving oneself to being passive." [5] It indicates an act of the will in which a person submissively empties himself and opens himself up to outside influence. " 'Having been swept and having been set in order' belong together and picture this house (man) as having been made ready for a tenant." [6] These three terms aptly portray the meditative state that mediums, witches, and other agents of the occult must achieve before their control spirits will come upon them. Drugs, music, lighting effects, and a variety of other methods are used to move a man's will to this state prepared for spirit world operation. When a man allows himself to be in this concentrated state he is up for grabs in the spirit world. He opens himself to occult influence, whether he is conscious of it or not!

John learned this lesson in a frightening way just two days after he trusted in the Lord Jesus. He had been on drugs for two years before I met him. Although he had experienced some "beautiful" things on his drug trips, he felt certain there was something missing in his life. He talked of an LSD trip as "going to see God." Even though he had seen what he called God many times on trips, he realized that he had never come to know God in a personal way through Jesus Christ. As the Good News was shared with him, he eagerly placed his faith in the God-Man, Jesus Christ. Contrary to my advice, two days later John went on another LSD trip. Everything proceeded as it always had—the walls waved, all was in motion, and an old white-haired man was sitting before him sending forth vibrations of peace and love. Suddenly the walls clapped together and opened up to a new, horrifying scene. Instead of the old man sitting before him, three demon-like creatures hurled lightning bolts at him. He feared he would die because of their attack. Then he remembered that he had received the Lord Jesus Christ into his heart and this thought dismissed the awful scene confronting him.

John's terrible experience illustrates graphically what the Apostle Paul expressed as he listed the spiritual armor needed for battle in the spirit realm. He says, " . . . in addition to all, taking up the shield of faith with which you will be able to extinguish all the flaming missiles (fiery darts or lightning bolts) of the evil one" (Ephesians 6:16, parentheses added).

Beware of permitting yourself to be in an elevated, meditative state, open to spirit world influence. Whether you move into this state by natural means or by the use of artificial devices, there is no guarantee who is in control at that level. "All things are lawful for me, but not all things are profitable. All things are lawful for me, but I will not be mastered (allow myself to be brought under the authority) by anything" (I Corinthians 6:12, parentheses added).

(6) *Many occult practices create a strange magnetism coupled with an underlying fear in the participant.* Many of my counselees tell of craving the powers, knowledge, and feeling the occult gives: "I desire it, but it scares me so!" Linda was one example, a single working girl who always had been fascinated with the occult. She found herself controlled by a spirit after yielding through an emotional crisis in her life. Linda had been notified that her fiance, David, had been killed in action in Viet Nam. A few days later she received a poem from David that he had written just before his death. Naturally she cherished it, and after consulting the ouija board, decided to tack it on the inside of her closet door. Within a week she began to reveal to her roommates that David's spirit lived in her closet: "He tells me what to do and what not to do. I like it, but for some reason he scares me!" The roommates brushed this aside as

pure fantasy caused by her deep sorrow, until one evening they found Linda shaking with fear from what David's spirit had told her to do. Immediately all three girls consulted the ouija board: it said that Linda should burn the poem. She vehemently refused to burn the last word from her lover, and after she had calmed down they all retired for the night. About 12:20 a.m. the roommates heard a terrible scream from Linda's bedroom. They rushed in, turned on the light, and were shocked at the scene—the closet door had been ripped off its hinges! It was an incredible sight! Linda finally settled down, jumped out of bed, and burned the poem. Now Linda will tell you that David's spirit lives inside her: "He tells me what to do and what not to do. I like it, but it scares me so!"

The occult is remarkably fascinating, yet this fascination is a trap set by Satan and his evil spirits. No matter how good it looks, how appealing it is, or how harmless it seems, the occult is dangerous. Millions of people have opened themselves up to the powers of darkness through fascination with the occult.

## THE RELIGIOUS TRAP

The religious trap is by far Satan's most effective trap. It makes full use of the occult, wrapping it in a religious package. Therefore it has the benefits of both: the alluring power of the occult and the respectability of the religious. Many people would not think of tampering with the occult, but put a religious cloak over it, claim it is from God, quote some Bible verses, and the religious trap is set.

Paul warns "that in later times some will fall away from the faith, paying attention to deceitful spirits and doctrines of demons . . . " (I Timothy 4:1). He strikes at the energizing source behind false teachers mentioned so frequently in the Bible—the subtle deception of false doctrine comes from Satan's evil spirits. Much of the false teaching today obviously is not centered on the God of the Bible, such as that from Anton Lavey's Satan Church, from cults that revolve around traditional church heresies, and from religions of the world that are not based on the Christian Bible.

This false teaching poses minor problems compared to that coming from false teachers within the framework of professing Christianity. The spirits that deceive this latter group of teachers shrewdly camouflage their work inside the camp of Christianity. The Bible presents four significant characteristics of the false teachers that these spirits work through. Paul explains to Timothy that "evil men and imposters will proceed from bad to worse, deceiving and being deceived" (II Timothy 3:13). It is important to know that all of these characteristics might not be found in one person.

(1) *They profess to be believers.* Paul speaks to this issue in II Corinthians 11:13-15:

> For such men are false apostles, deceitful workers, disguising themselves as apostles of Christ.

> And no wonder, for even Satan disguises himself as an angel of light.

> Therefore it is not surprising if his servants also disguise themselves as servants of righteousness; whose end shall be according to their deeds.

These are not men who worship the devil and pretend to be servants of righteousness; they actually believe they are servants of righteousness because of the deception of the spirits. These men will be shocked when they stand before the Lord at the judgment saying, "Lord, Lord, did we not do many things in your name?" The Lord will then "declare to them, 'I never knew you; depart from me, you who practice lawlessness' " (Matthew 7:23).

(2) *They act in the name of Jesus.* At that same judg-

ment setting Jesus tells us what the false teachers will say in their defense:

> Many will say to me on that day, 'Lord, Lord, did we not prophesy in your name, and in your name cast out demons, and in your name perform many miracles?' (Matthew 7:22)

Their first claim is that they have spoken, and possibly even predicted in Jesus' name. Some of the false teachers will be preachers and Bible teachers—all who have spoken in the name of the Lord. Jesus warns us earlier in this chapter to "Beware of the false prophets, who come to you in sheep's clothing, but inwardly are ravenous wolves" (Matthew 7:15). Speaking in the name of the Lord is part of the "sheep's clothing" that disguises these "ravenous wolves."

A good example from Scripture of false teachers who speak in the name of Jesus is in II Corinthians ll. Paul was seriously concerned that the Corinthians whom he had led to Christ had been deceived by false teachers posing as servants of righteousness. Paul expressed his concern this way:

> For I am jealous for you with a godly jealousy; for I betrothed you to one husband, that to Christ I might present you as a pure virgin. But I am afraid, lest as the serpent deceived Eve by his craftiness, your minds should be led astray from the simplicity and purity of devotion to Christ. (II Cor. 11:2-3)

Paul feared that they had been led astray from their pure, single-minded devotion to the Lord Jesus Christ by Satan's craftiness. In verse 4 he tells them how they had been deceived so effectively:

> For if one comes and *preaches another Jesus* whom we have not preached, or you receive a *different spirit*

which you have not received, or a *different gospel* which you have not accepted, *you bear this beautifully.* (italics added)

Paul described the approach of these false teachers by using three interesting terms: another Jesus, different spirit, and different gospel. These follow in sequence: another Jesus is preached, thus a different spirit is received, and a different gospel is accepted. The word, another, is from the Greek word *allos,* meaning another of the same kind, though slightly different. So "another Jesus" refers to the same Jesus of Nazareth, but presents a little different picture of what he said and did while on the earth. These false preachers used his name and spoke of him, but their preaching was not portraying the true, biblical Jesus. Superficial reasons why they preached another Jesus might have been because of their preconceived ideas and misunderstandings, or just that they denied his lordship; the underlying reason was that Satan was slipping in his counterfeit of the Lord Jesus Christ—another Jesus. This preaching seemed to be right on, for the Corinthian believers did not notice anything strange or satanic about this Jesus. The teachers and the hearers both were totally deceived by the devil.

The next two terms explain the results of preaching another Jesus. "Different" is from the Greek word *heteros,* meaning another of an altogether different kind where the substance has been changed. What spirit had the Corinthians received? According to I Corinthians 12:12-13 they had received the Holy Spirit at the time of spiritual birth. What then is a spirit, altogether different, from the Holy Spirit— an unholy spirit? This verse says that through the preaching of false teachers the Corinthian believers actually received a "different spirit" and a "different gospel" than they had previously accepted. What was the gospel the Corinthians had previously received? It was the gospel of the grace of God. A "different gospel" would be "any denial or perversion of the gospel of the grace of God. Its essential stamp is that it denies the full efficacy of God's grace alone to save, keep and perfect, and introduces an element of human merit." [7] The Corinthian believers had acknowledged a different gospel as the genuine gospel; in other words, the counterfeit Jesus had been extremely effective.

Through several counseling experiences within Christian circles today I have witnessed some striking similarities to the situation in Corinth. On one occasion Mary, a college student, came to me after experiencing deep depression. As I inquired about her Christian experience, I found that she had received the Lord Jesus as her Savior at an early age, but that she had had a strange experience just six months prior to our meeting that proved to be the cause of her depression. Someone had explained to her that she needed to have the "baptism of the Holy Spirit." Naturally desiring anything available to enable her to live the Christian life more victoriously, she went to a church service where she could receive this "baptism." When the minister called for those who had never received the baptism of the Holy Spirit, she was one of the first to go forward to the altar. There she prayed and opened herself for the "spirit" to come upon her. She pleaded with the Lord for a few minutes, then an unusual warmth came over her body, and she began to speak uncontrollably in what seemed to be another language. Everything was so beautiful, and she felt so good she knew it was of the Lord!

From previous counseling experiences I suspected that this spirit was a counterfeit. This was confirmed when she revealed that her depression had begun a few days after her baptism experience. It was very difficult to convince Mary that her beautiful experience could possibly have been from the devil. She finally understood the situation, prayed with me, and resisted that spirit. She is now free from the depression, and no longer speaks in tongues. Mary had been deceived by Satan, the angel of light, and had received a different spirit.

Many experiences similar to the one above have been witnessed by men around the world who counsel in the area of the demonic. One lady who received the baptism of the Holy Spirit asked a Christian pastor to test the spirit she had received. It was not the Holy Spirit, but rather an evil spirit by the name of Jesus. This is becoming a common occurrence—that a demon will call itself Jesus. Another girl, after receiving the baptism, was directed by that same spirit to stop her car on the way home and raise a cat from the dead—and the resurrection was successful! It is difficult for me to believe the Holy Spirit works in this way because it simply is not consistent with what we know from the Bible of his work.

The sad thing is that, just as the Corinthians accepted freely these counterfeit works of the devil ("you bear this beautifully," II Cor. 11:4), so there are many believers today who eagerly accept anything that speaks of Jesus or anyone who speaks in the name of Jesus.

The second claim false teachers make in their defense is that they cast out demons in the name of the Lord Jesus. Many people use this as conclusive evidence that a person's work is of the Lord, supporting this belief from Jesus' experience with the Pharisees in Matthew 12. After Jesus healed a demon-possessed man who was blind and dumb, the Pharisees accused him of casting out the demons by the power of Satan. The Lord replied:

. . . Any kingdom divided against itself is laid waste; and any city or house divided against itself shall not stand.

And if Satan casts out Satan, he is divided against himself; how then shall his kingdom stand? (Matthew 12:25-26)

At first glance the words of Jesus seem to suggest that Satan would not cast out one of his evil spirits, but this is not the whole picture. Dr. Merrill F. Unger significantly contributes to understanding this point when he says:

> Upon closer scrutiny, however, it will be discovered that Jesus's reference is solely to the *hostile* invasion of the kingdom of darkness by the actual and effectual power of light, *wherein Satan suffers real and permanent injury.* There is no allusion to Satan's own deceptive, and seemingly self-injurious methods, which are but a feint to extend his power and sway. Jesus is certainly not denying the power of the prince of the demons to allocate his satellites where he sees fit, or to effect their removal from a particular abode, if only temporarily (Matt. 12:43-45), to deceive, to excite fear and dread, and to inspire demon worship. Such expulsions are *not* divisions in the Satanic kingdom, nor Satan casting out himself, but keen Satanic strategy and diabolic miracle to build up and spread out the empire of evil.[8]

I am convinced that much casting out of demons we witness today does no more than open the door to more extensive demonic control in a person's life. The release is only temporary!

One final claim made by false teachers is that they perform many miracles in the name of Jesus. Miracles is from the Greek term *dunamis,* and is "used with reference to a 'work of power,' here including all works that seem to require supernatural power."[9] Here we have unbelievers who profess to be believers in Christ, performing various supernatural acts. Jesus gives us additional teaching about the miracles of these false teachers. In Matthew 24:24 he says that in the last days before he returns to the earth "false prophets will arise and will show great signs and wonders, so as to mislead, if possible, even the elect." Although signs and wonders are terms used with *dunamis* to describe the miracles of the Lord Jesus, these three terms are also used to speak of the Antichrist's power which is given to him by Satan. Since false teachers are forerunners of the Antichrist, it is no surprise that they are able to exercise great signs, wonders, and works of power (*dunamis*).

Through the deception of the occult, false teachers may receive occult powers unknowingly, believing these powers are the supernatural gift of God. This is obvious in the astounding case of a Mexican peasant woman I interviewed, who I will call Carlita. Carlita first noticed she possessed healing power when she was able to cure animals in the circus where she had worked all her life. This continued for some time until one afternoon a spirit by the name of Hermanito Cuauhtemoc came upon her. He explained to Carlita that he was sent by God to heal people through her. She accepted the opportunity to be used by God in this way; and Cuauhtemoc has now been healing people through Carlita for nearly fifty years.

Carlita's healings are strange! She does not pray over a person asking God to heal them—she actually operates on people with a dull hunting knife! Over the past fifty years she has performed every kind of operation imaginable—on the heart, the back, the eyes, etc. A medical doctor who had observed Carlita perform many operations was present when I interviewed her. He told of one case where Carlita cut into a person's chest cavity, took the heart out for examination, and handed it to him. After she closed the person up, without stitches, she suggested that he go to his hotel room and rest for three days. When the three days were up he left Mexico City, a healthy man, with no scars from the surgery. I asked the doctor what explanation he could give for such an amazing work. He replied, "There is no explanation medically. It's a miracle!"

The remarkable thing about Carlita's work is that she always operates in a dark room with her eyes shut. The reason for this is that Carlita does not do the operations herself—

Hermanito Cuauhtemoc acts through her. When he takes over her body, her eyes close and he speaks and acts through her—he has total control. One intelligent, mature man from the United States was skeptical when he went to view an operation for the second time. Cuauhtemoc sensed that the man did not believe, so he took the man's hand on the operating table and made him take out a tumor that was in the person's back. This man is no longer a skeptic! He told me, "I don't care if it is God's power or Satan's, because it is real and people are being helped through it."

Carlita's ministry comes from a sincere heart; she gives all of the glory to God who she believes sent Cuauhtemoc to work these mighty acts of power through her. Nevertheless, she is being deceived. Carlita is a medium by her own admission, and it is Cuauhtemoc who is in control, not the Lord. He claims to be the spirit of the ancient Aztec Indian chief who now is chief of all the spirits in North America. He was sent by his "God" all right—Satan, the god of this world. Carlita is deceived by the false belief that everything supernatural must be from God, especially if it helps people. After talking with Carlita for two hours, and listening to Cuauhtemoc twice during the evening, I asked her the source of her power. She answered, "If not God, who else?"

Clear illustrations of "ministers of God" who use occult power to heal can be found among many modern day faith-healers. Dr. Kurt Koch's *Occult Bondage and Deliverance* cites many examples of mediumistic healings. He gives the example of one Bible preacher who exercised great powers, but inherited these powers from his parents who were mediums. He says of another popular faith-healer that "his power to heal is more indicative of a mediumistic ability than a gift of the Holy Spirit. It is possible that he originally received these mediumistic powers from the old Indian who once healed him in his younger days." [10]

When considering healing that possibly comes from demonic sources, many acts of power used by noted faith-healers today make me extremely cautious. One such act of power that concerns me most is called "being slain in the Spirit," or "being overcome by the power of the Spirit." This often takes place when the leader of a service asks people to come forward to the altar for healing or for other reasons. He meets a person at the altar, holds his hand over him or places it on his head, and repeats some spiritual words. Through an unseen force the person literally is struck down, immediately building his confidence in the power of the leader. The person is then more open to suggestions the leader makes about healing or spiritual issues. Is this from God or from the devil?

Aside from several counseling experiences clearly connected with demonic activity, I know at least two reasons why this powerful act is not of God. First, this demonstration of power is very common among various occult and spiritist groups throughout the world. (Some evidence of this was given in the film, *Witchcraft*: 1970.) It is a tool frequently used by the evil spirit world. Second, this demonstration of power is never mentioned in the Bible as a work of the Holy Spirit. When God slays a man he does not get back up to tell about it—he is dead! The burden of proof is on the one who uses this power to give evidence that it is from God. Remember, false teachers can also perform many miracles in the name of Jesus. This is not to say that all who exercise this power are false teachers; they could possibly be believers deceived by the great deceiver, Satan, the angel of light.

Satan is the most effective counterfeiter the world will ever know. He loves to give good experiences that make people feel spiritually high or to give them a sense of a supernatural power working in and through them—all in the name of Jesus!

(3) *False teachers will have many followers.* A popular, though incorrect, way to measure God's blessing is the "numbers game." That a teacher has many followers gives no conclusive evidence of God's approval of his ministry. This is not an accurate measure of what is of God, for the Lord said, "And many false prophets (teachers) will arise, and will mislead *many"* (Matthew 24:11, parentheses and italics added). Peter echoed the same warning when he said, "There will also be false teachers among you, who will secretly introduce destructive heresies . . . And *many will follow* their sensuality" (II Peter 2:1-2, italics added). Many will follow the false teachers because of the clever disguise the angel of light has cast upon them. Satan's description will be effective "so as to mislead, if possible, even the elect (the true believers)" (Matthew 24:24, parentheses added). Today there should be no surprise at movements and ministries with many followers that appear to be from God, but when examined biblically are found to be sources of demonic activity couched in much appealing truth. Numbers alone do not constitute a valid test of whether a ministry is of God because Satan's deceptive work will also have a great following.

(4) *God's Word is secondary to experience.* This general characteristic undergirds the religious trap! The Bible is viewed as a primer, but experience is ultimate. This low view of God's Word only leads to defeat in the Christian life and opens the door to demonic deception. Many people accept supernatural experiences as gifts from God with no Scriptural basis for such experiences. We are constantly warned by the Lord not to pay attention to anything or anybody not in agreement with the Word.

Isaiah warns,

To the law and to the testimony! If they do not speak according to this word (Word of God), it is because they have no dawn (light). . . . (Isaiah 8:20, parentheses added)

The Lord will not guide men into anything that is contrary or in addition to the Bible. This is why Paul was so concerned that the Corinthians who were spiritually immature, needing instruction about exercising charismatic gifts, learn *"not to exceed what is written"* (I Corinthians 4:6, italics added). John also spoke to this issue in light of the deceivers in the world:

> Watch yourselves, that you might not lose what we have accomplished, but that you may receive a full reward. *Anyone who goes too far and does not abide in the teaching of Christ* does not have God; the one who abides in the teachings, he has both the Father and the Son. (II John 8-9, italics added)

Although he speaks specifically about false teachers, John's words can easily be applied to false experiences as well. If your supernatural experience does not match up to the Word of God, then it is time to test it out. Satan loves nothing better than to give people overwhelming and thrilling experiences that seem to come from God. This is all part of the way he disguises himself as an angel of light to trap people into false religion. Many unsuspecting believers have sought something deeper from the Lord, and have received visions, powers of automatic writing, and charismatic gifts—all coming from the Counterfeiter.

Automatic writing has made an unusual hit in the Christian world. It is an ancient occult practice where a person sits at a desk and allows a spirit to guide his pen. The person may be in a trance, in a state of meditation, or simply listening to voices. Two anonymous women called "Two Listeners" wrote the book entitled *God Calling*. They claimed that the living Christ spoke to them personally, day after day, giving them this message as they waited with pen in hand for him to appear and speak. In the foreword of the book, one of the "Two Listeners" made this interesting statement:

> We felt all unworthy and overwhelmed by the wonder of it, and could hardly realize that *we* were being taught, trained and encouraged day by day by Him personally, when millions of souls, far worthier, *had to be content with guidance from the Bible.* . . .[11] (italics added)

These women were using nothing more than the occult technique of automatic writing. The book is full of good thoughts, but careful examination will show that many of the concepts sound as though they originate from the angel of light, rather than the Living Christ. This whole experience is inconsistent with God's Word, that is our only reliable guide to examining this kind of activity.

Taking the Bible second to religious experience is extremely popular in the charismatic movement. This is particularly true of the experience of speaking in tongues. Almost everyone agrees that there are three possible sources of this phenomenon: God, psychology, or Satan. The sad thing about most who experience speaking in tongues is that they accept, without question, this experience as coming from the Lord. When someone is asked how he knows whether the spirit he has received is from God, from Satan, or psychologically induced, he usually replies, "It makes me feel so good —I just know it is from God." Whatever our feelings or thoughts may tell us, John warns that we must test every spirit to see if it is from God (I John 4:1-4). How to test spirits will be discussed in chapter 3.

When Paul wrote to Timothy about the deception of Satan in the difficult times that will come in the last days, he pointed Timothy toward the Bible and assured him that it would supply all his needs to be a man of God:

But evil men and imposters will proceed from bad to worse, *deceiving and being deceived.* You, however, continue in the things you have learned and become convinced of, knowing from whom you have learned them; and that from childhood you have known the sacred writings which are able to give you the wisdom that leads to salvation through faith which is in Christ Jesus. All Scripture is inspired by God and profitable for teaching, for reproof, for correction, for training in righteousness; *that the man of God may be adequate, equipped for every good work.* (II Timothy 3:13-17, italics added)

Notice that the only experience mentioned by Paul is that which comes out of God's Word. All extra-biblical experiences and those that do not obey biblical instructions should be rejected. Satan can use these forms of religious experience to deceive us.

### The Sin Trap

The effects of this trap are universal—because all have sinned! Sin in its most fundamental sense is opposition to God and to his character. Sin has been passed on to all mankind, from the first sin of Lucifer, Satan, who pridefully asserted himself as sovereign in the universe in opposition to God, to Adam's sin of rebellion against God's clear plan. Man is sinful by nature! It isn't necessary to teach a child to lie or to rebel against authority—he will do these things naturally.

Satan not only is the originator, he is also the minister of sin. Everything that opposes God's commandments aligns itself with him. Sin is his business! He works to lure people's thoughts, attitudes, and actions into rebellion against God. The devil's work further consists of accusing people of their sin and forcing them to believe they must pay for it themselves. Paul declares that Satan, " . . . the god of this world, has blinded the minds of the unbelieving, that they might not see the light of the gospel" (II Corinthians 4:4).

This is the Good News—that Jesus has already paid for man's sin. Jesus came to destroy the activity of Satan. "The Son of God appeared for this purpose, that he might destroy the works of the devil" (I John 3:8b). How could those works be destroyed? The penalty for man's sin is death. Jesus died on the cross, taking the penalty of death for everyone. By simply accepting Christ's payment for sin, anyone can experience forgiveness and freedom from its penalty.

Before you can effectively deal with sin you must personally accept or trust in Christ's payment for it. His death on the cross is the basis for any kind of release from sin's subtle power—it has made full payment for our death penalty for sin, providing forgiveness for all our sin. Christ's death canceled out all of the devil's accusations against us and has disarmed him in order to destroy all of his works (Colossians 2:12-14). All of this is a free gift to you (Romans 6:23). A gift is not yours to enjoy until you personally accept it. This acceptance is what Jesus meant by the word believe. He put it simply when he said, "For God so loved the world that He gave His only begotten Son (Jesus), that whoever believes in Him should not perish (will not have to pay the death penalty for his own sin), but have eternal life (right now) (John 3:16, parentheses added). A person who recognizes himself or herself as a sinner, and his or her need to make payment for that sin, is in a perfect position to personally accept Christ's payment.

We see that the unbeliever has no choice but to be enslaved by sin because he has not chosen to accept Christ's gift of freedom from sin. And he cannot please God. On the other hand, the believer can choose whether he will operate in sin, rebelling against God, or whether he will act from his newborn spirit to obey God. As long as the believer acts from his newborn spirit, he enjoys his personal relationship with God through the Lord Jesus Christ; when he acts in sin, he is robbed of the *enjoyment* of that relationship. The enjoyment of our relationship with God, based on our continuing communication and trust in him, is called fellowship. John tells us that in order to enjoy our relationship with God after we have sinned, we must simply confess, or humbly acknowledge, our sins to him. This restores our fellowship with the Lord, but not our relationship. We cannot lose our relationship with the Lord; yet we may often be out of fellowship with him and therefore not able to enjoy our relationship. In a small way this is mirrored in a marriage. If my wife and I are at odds because of something I have done, at that moment we certainly are not *enjoying* our relationship, but we are still *related* to one another. When the wrong has been acknowledged, we can enjoy our relationship again.

*The sin trap involves neglect of this practice of confession or acknowledgment of sin in the believer's life.* It is clear from Scripture that habitual sin opens the door to demonic attack in the believer's life. Sin may simply be defined as disobedience to the revealed will of God either by commission, a voluntary action, or by omission, an act of neglect. The basic intent of sin opposes God. A believer who sins acts against God's purposes in favor of the devil. A believer involved in habitual or unconfessed sin is playing right into the hands of the enemy, and Satan will "take advantage of" him (II Corinthians 2:11).

Paul speaks specifically to this issue in Ephesians 4:26-27: "Be angry, and yet do not sin; do not let the sun go down on your anger, and *do not give* the devil an opportunity (a place)" (italics and parentheses added). It is interesting that the command not to give the devil a place in one's life is nestled in a paragraph dealing with habitual sin.

Paul strongly states that Satan's activity in a believer's life is triggered by habitual and unacknowledged sin.

The Bible is full of illustrations of this truth. The Lord explained to Peter that Satan was about to "sift him like wheat" (Luke 22:31), and he prayed that Peter's faith would not fail through this experience. Why did the Lord not stop Satan's work in Peter's life, instead of just offering prayer for him? Possibly Peter had already fallen into Satan's sin trap (Luke 22:31-34). Peter had been playing right into Satan's hands through his habitual sin of pride. What happened was inevitable. Paul warned Timothy not to allow a new convert to be placed in a position of spiritual leadership, "lest he become conceited (proud) and fall into the condemnation incurred by the devil" (I Timothy 3:6, parentheses added). Ananias sinned when he lied to the Lord about the sale of his property, and Satan gained control of him through it (Acts 5:3).

Many times a believer is unaware of how habitual sin opens the door to demonic activity and through ignorance fully cooperates with Satan. After harboring some sin for a period of time, a believer will come to a point where he is truly repentant and will confess the sin to God. In a few days he finds himself committing the very same sin again—and confessing it again. The cycle goes on—sin, confess, sin, confess, sin . . . . Frustrated and defeated, the believer begins to wonder how he can do such a thing, and yet be so repentant a few minutes later. Questioning his sincerity, he becomes negative and introspective. "Maybe the Christian life does not work for me?" "Maybe I'm not a believer in the first place?" Depression sets in and he is spiritually defeated.

There are at least two reasons why this believer has been wiped out. First, he may have a faulty understanding of the spiritual life (this will be discussed in chapter 2). Second, the believer may be ignorant of Satan's devices. He does not understand that his habitual sin has given Satan the opportunity to take hold of an area of his life. If Satan has trapped him through his sin, the poor believer can confess until he turns pale—and probably will—but the trap will not be released. Confession only deals with a man's willful sin, but the believer must deal with Satan in order to get out of this trap. If I were being choked by a bully right now, I would not start beating my own leg to make him quit; I would beat on the bully. In a similar way, Satan tricks people into believing that his activity is really nothing more than the product of sin in their own defeated lives. People do sin habitually, and that sin must be dealt with, but through that open door Satan is given a place in the believer's life and he must be handled as well. This is the sin trap that manifests itself in uncontrollable spiritual problems. However, this situation does not rule out the fact that uncontrollable spiritual problems also can be produced by an undisciplined life. Jerry was a good illustration of one who had been caught in the sin trap. He just could not gain the victory over his sinful problem—homosexuality. The filthy thought and periodically the act itself were dragging Jerry into suicidal depression in his new Christian life. It seemed like the more he fought the problem the worse it became. Just a few days before he came in for counseling he said he was actually "driven" to a park where he participated in more homosexuality. This problem had definitely become uncontrollable and he was afraid of what he might do next. He said, "If this is how I must live the rest of my life, I might as well end my life!" I assured him that I agreed with him. That night we dealt not only with Jerry's sin of yielding to homosexuality, but also with the demonic problem that was present because of his sin. It was a beautiful experience to witness a young man, deep in sin and enslaved by evil spirits, freed by the power of the Lord Jesus Christ!

Another example of a believer caught in the sin trap was

Carol. At the beginning of her junior year in college Carol had been overwhelmed with deep depression. She had visited one psychiatrist who was not much help, and had decided that a second one would not hurt. For many weeks Carol saw both psychiatrists. At least it was good, she felt, to have had someone who would listen; however, neither of the psychiatrists could help her. Her real problem escaped them, as Carol had a spiritual problem caused by Satanic influence. She came to me at the urging of her roommate, and as I listened and probed, it was clear that her depression stemmed from an unusual bitterness toward her parents and from guilt relating to sexual immorality. In Carol's case, Satan's demons were having a ball doing their thing—they encouraged her bitterness and accused her of sin. After a few hours of explanation about spiritual warfare, she confessed her sin, resisted the demonic harassment and determined in her mind to be more alert to the enemy's tactics. She is now doing beautifully in her Christian life—without deep depression and two psychiatrists.

When the sin trap is unveiled with all its devastation, sin becomes a more serious matter. Not that we should become paranoid concerning it by praying over a daily sin list, but we should be more sensitive to sin. Playing with sin is not a spiritual game; it is opening the door to a fierce enemy, Satan—who plays for keeps.

## THE FACETS OF ATTACK

The enemy's spiritual traps can be more fully understood by explaining the fronts, focus, degrees, and symptoms of his attack.

(1) *Fronts of Attack.* It is important to realize that there is more than one battle front to guard in spiritual warfare. Christians have been keeping a close watch diligently on one front, only to have been demolished from the rear. Paul

identifies three battle fronts from which Satan attacks believers; in order to be triumphant in this warfare we must cover each of these fronts adequately. Victory on two of the three fronts, leaving the third unattended, still leaves open a front where Satan can do significant damage. These three fronts are listed and briefly described in Ephesians 2:1-3:

> And you were dead in your trespasses and sins, in which you formerly walked according to the course of this *world,* according to the *prince of the power of the air,* of the spirit that is now working in the sons of disobedience. Among them we too all formerly lived in the lusts of our *flesh,* indulging the desires of the flesh and of the mind, and were by nature children of wrath, even as the rest. (italics added)

Paul is contrasting the former position of the believer with his present position. In verses 1-3 he describes our position before God entered the picture. Verses 5-6 tell how God rescued us: "But God, being rich in mercy, because of his great love with which he loved us, even when we were dead in our transgressions, made us alive together with Christ" (by grace have we been saved). Unbelievers are subjected to these conditions without hope because they are without God. Yet believers, whose hope is from God, must still constantly be alert to the problem of sliding back into subjection to one or all of these areas—the world, the devil, and the flesh.

Our first battle front is the world. The *Oxford English Dictionary* tells us the world is "worldly affairs; the aggregate of things earthly; the whole circle of earthly goods, endowments, riches, advantages, pleasures, etc., which, although hollow and frail and fleeting, stir desire, seduce from God, and are obstacles to the cause of Christ." [12] To walk "according to the course of this world" (Ephesians 2:2) means to live "according to the ruling principles, or spirit of the world." [13] To walk "according to the course of this world" is to be in harmony with the world's norm that has been debased and corrupt since the fall of man. This is the same idea that Paul expressed in Romans 12:2 where he said, "Do not be conformed to this world." It is right to live in the world, it is wrong to be molded and preoccupied by it.

The world system is that context in which the believer must walk, without being fitted into its mold. Yet it acts as magnet, constantly drawing and enticing him toward greater involvement. Everything that makes up the world system is not necessarily evil in itself. Because the world is based upon its own temporal value system, it is diametrically opposed to God's eternal value system. To be caught up in the "course of this world" is to turn your back on the Lord. John speaks to this truth in I John 2:15-17:

> Do not love the world, nor the things in the world. If anyone loves the world, the love of the Father is not in him. For all that is in the world, the lust of the flesh and the lust of the eyes and the boastful pride of life, is not from the Father, but is from the world. And the world is passing away, and also its lusts; but the one who does the will of God abides forever.

It makes no difference what is someone's "world"—whatever is from the spirit of this age that keeps him from the Lord is dead wrong!

The second battle front is against "the prince of the power of the air, the spirit that is now working in the sons of disobedience" (Ephesians 2:2). This phrase obviously refers to Satan. In John 12:31, 14:30, and 16:11 he is called "the ruler of this world"; in Matthew 9:34 and 12:24 the Pharisees attribute Christ's miracles to Beelzebub, the prince of the demons. Satan is portrayed in these verses as a mighty, supernatural power ruling in two spheres: "the air, and abode of evil spirits; and the earth, the abode of unregenerate men. This prince is the No. 1 public enemy of the whole universe." [14] Satan energizes acts of disobedience through those who oppose God. These people are "sons like their fathers; together they second the disobedience of Adam, into which Satan lured him." [15]

In Ephesians 2:3 Paul speaks of the third battle front—the flesh. The flesh is a metaphorical term that explains the sin principle in a person's life. The capacity to sin arises from man's nature, inherited from Adam's first sin. We have seen that the unbeliever's flesh so dominates his will that he has no choice but to carry out its desires as Paul claims, "Among them we too all formerly lived in the lusts of our flesh, indulging the desires of the flesh" (Ephesians 2:3). On the other hand, the believer is set free from the domination of the flesh and has a new capacity to follow God. This new capacity is called his new nature or his reborn spirit. Although the flesh is no longer in control of the believer's will, it still is in him, always ready to operate when it gets a chance.

Just as the world, the flesh from inside the believer also acts as a magnet drawing him to sin. The results of yielding to these enticing vibes from the flesh are common.

Now the deeds of the flesh are evident, which are: immorality, impurity, sensuality, idolatry, sorcery, enmities, strife, jealousy, outbursts of anger, disputes, dissentions, factions, envyings, drunkenness, carousings, and things like these. . . . (Galatians 5:19-21)

All three battle fronts are cause for our great concern and deserve constant attention. The world has its lusts which draw the believer like a strong magnet from the outside; the flesh has its magnetic lusts pulling from within. In both cases, Satan provides the energy for attack. He is using the world's lusts and obstacles, while working unceasingly to stir up the lusts of the flesh—all in an effort to destroy God's work in and through man. In *Invisible War* Dr. Barnhouse illustrates these three fronts of attack:

> Each branch of warfare has its own defense and when the enemy strikes, he must be met by the defense that is suitable to his attack. Saboteurs are sought by the F.B.I., submarines are searched out by planes and destroyers to be finished off with depth charges, while aircraft must be located by radar and pursued by faster craft. To misjudge the course of any attack, or to attempt a defense against one thrust with means adapted to meet another is to risk harsh defeat.[16]

(2) *Focus of Attack.* We must recognize that the main focus of Satan's attack is the mind. We are told that his attack on unbelievers is through "blinding their minds" to the gospel of the Lord Jesus Christ (II Corinthians 4:4). In the case of the believer, Satan frequently shoots thoughts into the mind that are destructive, aimed against the things of God and our relationship with him. In II Corinthians 10:3-6 Paul explains that in spiritual warfare we are "destroying speculations and every lofty thing raised up against the knowledge of God, and taking every thought captive to the obedience of Christ." We must destroy or reject any reasoning that enters our minds against God. We must also take "every thought captive to the obedience of Christ." The word "thought" is from the same Greek word used for Satan's devices—we must capture every device of Satan that enters the mind for the purpose of obeying him and replace it with obedience to Christ. The origin of thoughts that Satan hurls into the mind is usually obvious. The problem is that believers have a hard time realizing that Satan actually does work in this way.

Satan frequently shoots thoughts into the mind that are deceptive, cloaked in the name of God. Paul was concerned about this in II Corinthians 11:3 when he said:

But I am afraid, lest as the serpent deceived Eve by his craftiness, *your minds should be led astray* from the simplicity and purity of devotion to Christ. (italics added)

Even for this kind of attack, that is deceptive and concealed in a religious context, discernment is available, but only if we are aware that Satan works in this way.

Satan makes use of all three battle fronts when focusing his attack on the mind. The world provides an infinite number of tools for Satan's use, including everything communicated through the five senses. He fills the mind with all kinds of worthless paraphernalia from the world, in turn stirring up the lusts of the flesh. If this combination does not bring a person nearer to one of his traps, then he sends direct thoughts of his own to trip him up.

(3) *Degrees of Attack.* There is so much confusion and misunderstanding about the extent of Satan's activity in a believer's life. Most of this perplexity can be alleviated by properly understanding the term demon-possession. This term does not appear in the Bible. The word that is translated as demon-possessed is the Greek verb *daimoni* which means to be under the power or influence of a demon. This makes a great difference in how we answer the perpetual question, "Can a Christian be demon-possessed?" If you mean can a Christian be *owned* by an evil spirit, the answer unquestionably is no! The Christian is owned or possessed by God, "for he has been bought with a price . . . " (I Corinthians 6:20). But if you mean can a Christian be under the power or influence of an evil spirit, the answer assuredly is yes! Another question that also pops up quite often is, "Can a Christian be indwelt by a demon?" Though I cannot prove conclusively that evil spirits are able to indwell believers, it is my opinion from experience that they do this to certain degrees. Nevertheless, whether the demons perform their wicked schemes from the inside or

the outside of a person makes little difference. The process of liberation is the same. To avoid emotional overtones and confusion we will not use demon-possession to describe Satan's activity, nor will we be concerned whether demons operate inside or outside of a man. Rather, we will define the degrees of demonizing (*daimonizomai,* Greek).

There are three progressive degrees of attack. Each of these degrees overlaps the other; it is extremely difficult, if not impossible, to discern when one degree of demonic influence progresses into another. The encouraging thing is that the same strategy for fighting demons applies to all three degrees of attack.

The first degree of attack is harassment. This is the weakest of Satan's three attacks. Because he has not been given a place in a person's life through one of his traps, there is very little he can do. At this level he can thwart or hinder the efforts of believers by throwing various obstacles in their paths (I Thessalonians 2:18; Romans 15:22), such as shooting destructive and deceptive thoughts in believers' minds (II Corinthians 10:3-6; 11:3). Good pictures of Satan's harassment are the fiery darts in Ephesians 6:16 and the roaring lion in I Peter 5:8. All of these, and more, are ways Satan harasses. The chief work of demons in harassment is to throw incessant accusations against a person. A constant barrage of condemning thoughts piles up the guilt so high the person can't see out.

The second degree of attack is influence. This has a stronger effect than harassment, for here Satan has been given a place in the believer's life. This usually comes by giving in to Satan's harassment, from believing Satan and not the Lord. At this level the believer is playing right into the enemy's hands, and in some areas can be more influenced by Satan than by the Lord.

Peter clearly illustrates a believer influenced by Satan. After Jesus had experienced another encounter with the

Pharisees he took his disciples across the Sea of Galilee for a time of disciple-building. He taught them about false doctrine, and he asked them who people were saying he was. Peter rallied to the occasion by saying, "Thou art the Christ, the Son of the living God" (Matthew 16:16). Jesus commended this answer and revealed to them his intention to build his church on the very testimony that Peter had just spoken. Then the following conversation between Peter and the Lord took place:

> From that time Jesus Christ began to show His disciples that He must go to Jerusalem, and suffer many things from the elders and chief priests and scribes, and be killed, and be raised up on the third day. And Peter took Him aside and began to rebuke Him, saying, "God forbid it, Lord! This shall never happen to You." *But He turned and said to Peter, "Get behind Me, Satan! You are a stumbling-block to Me; for you are not setting your mind on God's interests, but man's.* (Matthew 16:21-23, italics added)

What a contrast to Peter's previous conversation with Jesus!

After Peter's rebuke to the Lord, Jesus bursts out with strange words—"Get behind Me, Satan!" Now we must assume that Jesus knew Peter's name and that this was not simply a slip of the tongue on Jesus' part.[17] I think it is clear that Jesus recognized that Satan was using Peter to trap him. Peter was renewing the wilderness temptation—to get Jesus to take a short cut to his throne by acting in independence rather than in dependence upon the Father. As soon as he recognized the Satanic influence, Jesus spoke the same words he used in the wilderness—"Get behind Me, Satan!" Jesus continued his rebuke of Peter by telling him that he was a stumbling block to him. Stumbling block is from the Greek word *skandalen* which was "originally the name of the part of a trap to which the bait was attached, hence, the trap or snare itself. . . ."[18] Just a few minutes before this incident Peter was blessed by the Lord, but now he stands rebuked because of Satanic influence in his life. Dr. Robertson puts it well:

> Thou art not, as before, a noble block, lying in its right position as a massive foundation stone. On the contrary, thou art like a stone quite out of its proper place, and lying right across the road in which I must go— lying as a stone of stumbling.[19]

Another illustration of believers under the influence of Satan is from Luke 22:31-34. During a time of training for the twelve at the last Passover meal, Jesus was teaching some last minute truths concerning the Kingdom of God and his approaching death. He again foretold his betrayal, and then settled an argument among the disciples as to who among them would be the greatest in the kingdom. This foolish and sinful discussion showed that the disciples were thinking more of themselves than ever before. Jesus rebuked them for their pride. Addressing Peter he said, "Simon, Simon, behold Satan hath desired to have you, that he may *sift you as wheat*" (Luke 22:31, italics added). In other words Satan wanted to influence or control these believers, and apparently they had opened the door for him to do so. Jesus went on to explain that this "sifting like wheat" in Peter's case would be his repeated denial of the Lord.

The third degree of demonic attack is control. This is the strongest degree of attack and is difficult to distinguish from demonic influence. It is possible that both of the above illustrations could be considered as control. When a person is controlled by Satanic forces the control is normally restricted to certain areas of his life at certain times rather than exhibited by total control all of the time. Demonic control usually takes place when a person opens one or more areas of his life widely and habitually to evil spirits.

A clear illustration of demonic control is given in Acts 5. Ananias and Sapphira had not confessed their sin to the Lord. Peter asked, "Ananias, why has Satan *filled* your heart to lie to the Holy Spirit, and to keep back some of the price of the land?" (Acts 5:3, italics added). It is interesting to note that Peter used the Greek word *pleroo,* which can also be translated as filled or controlled. In other words, Peter asked, "Why has Satan *controlled* your heart . . . ?" Here we have a believer who had the Holy Spirit living in him permanently; yet he was somehow controlled by Satan to lie to God.

These three degrees of attack—harassment, influence, and control—span the range of demonic activity, demonizing, in a believer's life.

(4) *Symptoms of Attack.* It is important to recognize the universal effect Satan has on all unbelievers. Satan is described as "the spirit who now works in the sons of disobedience" (Ephesians 2:2). The Bible says more about the blinding effect of Satan in II Corinthians 4:3, 4:

> And even if our gospel is veiled, it is veiled to those who are perishing, in whose case the god of this world has blinded the minds of the unbelieving, that they might not see the light of the gospel of the glory of Christ, who is the image of God.

This blinding is the basic cause of many bizarre actions of unbelievers. The Hare Krishna devotees, with their unusual dress and chanting, are a good example of Satanic blindness. The significant thing to remember about such groups is that this blindness may have abnormal effects that do not give any direct clues to present Satanic influence or control.

A man's spirit is either dead or alive toward God. At physical birth his spirit is dead toward God because of his sinful nature; it cannot be alive toward God until a spiritual birth takes place through faith in Jesus Christ. This is not to say that a spirit that is dead toward God cannot function. Every unbeliever has a spirit that is very much alive, but as far as his contact with God, his spirit is dead. He cannot communicate with God, please him, or have a relationship with him. This is what Jesus explained to Nicodemus: "That which is born of the flesh is flesh; and that which is born of the Spirit is spirit" (John 3:6). So for man to have contact with God, he must have a reborn spirit—a spirit that is alive toward God.

It is through the spiritual part of man, alive or dead toward God, that demonic activity operates. This does not mean that all spiritual problems are demonic by any means. Many spiritual problems are the result of violations of biblical principles. Nor does this mean that demons only affect man's spirit, for they commonly affect the physical area as well.

Physical and spiritual problems are interlocked much of the time, but they can be separate from one another. People do have genuine physical problems that are not related to spiritual or demonic problems. Conversely, people do have genuine spiritual problems unrelated to the physical. Some have gone to extremes in this area by attributing nearly everything—both the physical and spiritual—to demons. It is certainly true that Satan's demons are the cause of many spiritual and physical problems, but *not all of them.* This extreme is part of the "when in doubt, cast it out" philosophy. Even though Satan is not the cause of every kind of physical and spiritual problem, he is enthusiastic about them and will use these problems to his advantage.

Satan's forces are capable of counterfeiting every symptom caused by other real physical and spiritual problems. Therefore, to list symptoms of all possible demonic attack would take forever; however, there are some common symptoms that are helpful to recognizing the work of demons in a person's life. For the most part these are taken from biblical accounts, verified by my own experience in counseling. Keep in mind that these symptoms cannot always be viewed as demonic—just because one has a few of these characteristics does not mean he is demonized. These symptoms, as they are described below, act only as *indicators* of possible demonic harassment, influence and control. They should not be used as an absolute catalogue of demonic symptoms. *Do not become a demon inspector!*

*Deep Depression.* This is the most common symptom of demonic attack. Obviously, depression is also caused by numerous physical and spiritual problems. It may simply mean that a person needs more sleep. A student prone to extreme introspection complained of heavy depression during a tough semester in his studies. He felt certain it was demonic, but because no other symptoms indicated the same I suggested that he change his sleeping habits from between three and four to seven or eight hours per night. The result? No more depression.

A girl came for counsel, confident that she was under the control of demons due to the depression she was experiencing. During our first session it came out that she had been to see many doctors about her problem. Each of these specialists diagnosed her problem as a physical disease which commonly causes deep depression. She simply was unable to accept their findings. There is no doubt in my mind that Satan and his evil spirits were excited about her problems and were definitely involved in some harassment, but her depression was caused by physical sickness.

Demonic depression most usually can be described in two ways. (1) A person is depressed over something he has done wrong, and evil spirits intensify the depression to an unbearable point. This intensification is brought about by heaping accusations against him from his past. Naturally, these accusations induce guilt feelings. Often the Christian interprets these as the conviction of the Holy Spirit. But the Holy Spirit does not accuse us of anything; he convicts or persuades us concerning sin, righteousness, and judgment (John 16:9-11). When a believer is convicted of some sin, he will have godly sorrow "which produces repentance (leading to salvation and deliverance)" (II Corinthians 7:10, parentheses added). But if a believer is bombarded with accusations (Colossians 2:13-15), he will have worldly sorrow and "the sorrow of the world produces death" (II Corinthians 7:10). When a believer has this kind of worldly sorrow, producing death (condemnation and spiritual destruction) you can count on it—there are demons involved. In the same light if there is any lingering guilt after dealing with sin before God, it is normally some kind of demonic harassment. The only exception to this is a misunderstanding of God's forgiveness and grace.

(2) Another form of demonic depression is what many call a dark cloud of depression. This is described as a sense of evil and darkness that overwhelms a person until he or she has no desire to live or to act normally. This depression is accompanied by great fear and much anxiety.

*Self Reproach:* This is directly connected to the accusing work of demons. It occurs when someone becomes completely discouraged with himself. His self-image is shattered, because he believes he can do nothing well and is worthless. This is such a common problem today. The problem of a poor self-image, whether or not it is from demonic influence, needs to be treated from God's Word. However, there is a point when this problem can become more serious. Usually when voices remind one of past sins or constantly condemn one's actions, demons are involved. With these thoughts rushing through the mind, a person begins to condemn himself verbally as well as through his attitude.

One girl heard a voice that did nothing but laugh at her

all of the time. She could hardly do anything without a condemning thought popping into her mind. When she went to Bible study or to church, the thought would occur to her, "How can you sit here with a straight face, acting like you are so saintly, with the things you have done, you hypocrite?" When she tried to pray, the thought would come, "You sure are not a very good example of a Christian with all the sin you have committed." Accusations were constantly being thrown against her concerning past sins she had already confessed. She began to think maybe she really did not mean it when she had confessed the sins before, so she tried it again. She still had no release from the overwhelming guilt. After going through this cycle too many times, she simply gave up, thinking, "The Christian life just does not work for me" and "I think possibly I am too wicked for the Lord to forgive." Demons had convinced her that she was completely worthless. It was so sad for me to hear how she had totally rejected herself. Assured that she had really trusted in the Lord as her Saviour, I suggested this dreadful problem she was experiencing could possibly have been caused by demonic harassment. We dealt with her problem along those lines; after a few hours of going through the Scriptures and then resisting any demonic activity in her life, she was a different girl! It was like a cloud had been lifted —the pressure was off! Now when defeating thoughts come to mind, she knows their source and resists them, knowing they are the lies of demons.

*Suicidal Thoughts and Attempts:* This symptom follows on the heels of deep depression and self-reproach. When these symptoms become so bad, many feel that ending it all is the easiest way to relieve pain. On the day that he came to see me one man was driven to get a knife to kill himself; he struggled against this force all the way to my office. After dealing with all demonic activity in his life, he gained relief from this problem for good. It is not that he will never be bothered by this drive again, but now he knows what to do to handle it himself. Satan's hate for people is real; he sends demonic forces to destroy and devour all that he can. In each of the suicidal cases I have counseled, the person had opened the door to demonic attack—at least to the point of harassment.

*Anti-Social and Passive Behavior:* Obviously this is a symptom that can easily be seen in scores of people not under any demonic oppression. However, this is a common characteristic of those influenced by demons. So often these persons hate and even fear being around others—especially believers in the Lord Jesus Christ. In its extreme form this passivism is a trance-like mannerism. Not long ago a girl came in for counseling about growth in the Christian life. While we were talking she simply flipped into a trance— staring off into space. As I questioned her in that state she stammered out vague answers or "I don't know." Then she began to talk irrationally, while still in the trance. Later we found out that she had been caught in the occult years ago, and had even gone into worshipping and praying to Satan.

*Uncontrollable Problems:* This shows up in so many ways. A believer sins, opening the door to demonic activity, and then he cannot quit that sin. Examples of this I have already given are the homosexual who was driven to the park and the man who was driven to kill himself. This demonic problem should not be mistaken for a person's lack of self-control of self-discipline.

Not only does this problem manifest itself in uncontrollable sin but also in unusual effects on a person. One woman with such a demonic problem was not able to sleep for days at a time and yet could still function well enough to be an efficient secretary.

*Immorality:* Sexual sin is one of Satan's favorite and most popular devices in this century. It is usually manifest in an abnormal desire for sex. One of the most bizarre cases I have seen was that of a girl who had intense fear and hate for sex. Even the thought of sexual intercourse made her sick —yet she had an unusual craving for it. This was one of the symptoms that helped to indicate a demonic problem in her life. Unknown to her friends, she had been a Satan worshipper for many years.

Immorality includes the deepest of all sexual sins, homosexuality. It is important to remember that sin is committed first, then demons rush in to do their work. They will harass with accusations and pile up guilt until one thinks he cannot be forgiven. When one is defeated at this level he often returns to more of the same sin. The demons' position begins to influence and eventually to control him. Without exception, in all of the homosexual cases I have worked with there have been some demonic activities involved. It is usually at the level of demonic harassment. Again, this is not to say that demons create the homosexual; however, after one gets involved in this sin the demons are right there for action. This is probably true for most sins, but especially so for this one.

*Unusual Bitterness, Temper, etc.:* When any of the deeds of the flesh are taken to extremes, there should be cause for suspicion about possible demonic sources. These actions, listed in Galatians 5:19-21, are: "immorality, impurity, sensuality, idolatry, sorcery, enmities, strife, jealousy, outbursts of anger, disputes, dissensions, factions, envyings, drunkenness, carousings, and things like these." A young man who came in for counseling about his dating experience expressed off hand that he had an unusually bad problem with his anger. He would throw things everywhere and become very destructive. At times he thought of killing the person who had triggered his anger. As we looked into other areas of his life there had been repeated contacts with the occult. After we had dealt with these areas of possible demonic oppression his raging temper ceased.

*Drugs:* People leave themselves wide open to demonic attack because of the mental passivity induced by drugs. Some have had wild, but beautiful, experiences from the use of drugs. A. E. Wilder Smith, head of the department of pharmacology at the University of Illinois Medical School, has pointed out that many of the experiences people have while on a drug trip cannot be explained in terms of biochemistry, but only by the supernatural. Drugs simply launch a person's mind and will uncontrollably into the spirit world. Any person involved in the use of drugs, legal or illegal, has opened the door to demonic attack.

*Great Strength and Power:* People under demonic control have been known to leap over high fences, and they sometimes fight off three or four men with their strength. This phenomenon often gives the clue to its demonic source.

*Psychic Power and Experience:* At one university a girl related how she was able to predict all kinds of things. She had known that her grandmother was going to die on a certain day, and had felt sharp pains when her mother was in an automobile accident. She could put spells on guys in order to get them to call her or not to call her. After realizing her powers, she began studying white witchcraft (casting good spells, as opposed to black witchcraft that involves evil spells). When someone has psychic tendencies, there is usually some occult connection either directly or indirectly through parents or friends. If an occult connection is discovered, it should be renounced as a tool of the devil, and the demons using it should be resisted. If there is no apparent connection to the occult, caution should still be taken to resist any possible demonic association. (The action of resisting will be discussed in chapter 4.)

*Irritation During Prayer, Bible Reading, or Preaching:* This symptom arises at the levels of demonic influence and control. The first time I ever saw what I recognized to be a demonic case, was when a young man came to our church one Sunday who wanted to receive Christ as his Saviour. He had a glassy-eyed stare that was strange, but I didn't think much of it at that time. As I explained to him the Good News of salvation in Jesus Christ and how he could receive it, I suggested that he pray to invite Jesus Christ into his life, placing faith in Him. Up to this point there was nothing unusual about the situation. When I began to pray, this man began to shake, nearly into convulsions. That seemed unusual! As I kept praying, he continued to shake. Even after I finished he became worse. I remembered one minister saying when I was a young boy that you must pray in the name of the Lord Jesus, or claim the blood of the Lord Jesus, when you suspect that Satan is present. So I prayed again, asking the Lord to free this man from what ever was bothering him, in the name of the Lord Jesus Christ. At that moment the trembling man took a deep breath of relief—and so did I! In following contacts I learned that he had been a member of a "Christian" group that was working with all kinds of miraculous feats. It was clear that he had been caught by Satan in the religious trap. After renouncing all of that activity, he became relieved of many irritations in his life—he was free!

Another time I opened a counseling session in prayer with a girl who I suspected to be under demonic control. She shrilled and held her head in pain. When I asked what was wrong, she said she could not stand to hear people pray. During the next few hours I discovered some very interesting indications of demonic activity—her parents were mediums and she had been entangled in the occult from childhood.

Some people become violent when the Bible is read. As I was seeking to give biblical insight about a certain problem, opening up my Bible, a man became very uncomfortable and jittery. This nervousness turned into what could best be described as panic, while he denied there was anything wrong.

Again, it is important to note that there are people who do get upset at prayer, Bible reading, and preaching who are not demonized in any way. A person may be under the conviction of the Holy Spirit and quite upset about his sin, or he may be physically ill or very uncomfortable.

*Abnormal Physical Pressure:* This is a very common happening. An incredible pressure seems to come upon the person so that he or she cannot move and is accompanied by the fear of an evil presence. Everyone seems to describe it in the same way. This phenomenon has been used by evil spirits in order to deter people from learning more about Satan and his powers. It normally occurs at the harassment level of attack.

*Impulsiveness:* Certainly there are many people who are impulsive without the help of demons. However extreme impulsiveness is a common characteristic of demonization. A person affected by demons may make quick, irrational decisions that are major in his life, like quitting his job, moving out of town suddenly, getting married or divorced.

*Epilepsy:* Uncontrollable convulsions of any kind *can* be demonic. Because of some other indicators an epileptic at one university was regarded as influenced or controlled by demons. One day a professor had the opportunity to witness this student's attack. As she mentioned the Lord Jesus and his blood paid to forgive sin, the student blurted out all kinds of blasphemy, cursing, and filthy talk. This is definitely not normal epilepsy!

On another occasion, one lady threw herself down on the floor during a time of prayer, going into convulsions. After these quit she did not know what had happened. It was found out later that she was deeply involved in the occult and had begun praying to Satan and other spirits.

*Functional Sickness:* When a person has severe pains, without medical reasons, this may be a demonic problem. A man suffering from constant migraine headaches had every possible test run on him to determine the source of his problem. It was only after dealing with demonic elements that the man got release from his problem.

On one occasion a girl experienced a painful physical attack during a counseling session. She also heard screaming voices along with the attack, telling her to get out of my office and away from me because I would hurt her. When she told me this, I asked her to pray with me in the name of the Lord Jesus and together we would resist whatever this was. We did, and in a matter of minutes she was relieved of her pain.

It is a must to keep a perspective here, realizing that sources other than demons, such as emotional stress, can cause functional sickness.

*Voices Opposing God:* Especially voices in the mind that blaspheme God should definitely be suspected as demonic. One man heard voices relating homosexual thoughts about God, although he was not even a homosexual. The only thing that seemed to bring relief was to renew his mind with new thoughts from the Bible to resist the evil spirits.

*Obsession with Committing the Unpardonable Sin:* This problem is becoming more and more frequent in my counseling experience. The peak of false demonic accusations is that one cannot be forgiven—even by God. A man's eternal destiny rides on this one. If he is convinced that he is in that bad a condition, he gives up. It is a miserable situation when someone feels unable to be forgiven by God or to receive the gift of eternal life from the Lord.

Evil spirits receive a lot of assistance in convincing a person of the unpardonable sin through the teaching of believers who warn of this possibility. All of this stems from a misunderstanding of the context in which the passages occur that speak of this sin (Matthew 12:31-32, Mark 3:28-30,

Luke 12:10). The unpardonable sin was to stubbornly and knowledgeably deny the work of God which the Holy Spirit revealed in the perfect God-Man, Jesus Christ—to call him a work of Satan. This sin cannot happen today because the Holy Spirit does not have the perfect Man, Jesus Christ, through whom he works. This sin could only be committed in the time Jesus physically ministered on earth. Any obsession with committing the unpardonable sin, whether brought on by a misunderstanding of what the passages say or by misinformation, is absolutely invalid and must be rejected.

*Multiple Personality:* In this symptom a person may exhibit two or more different personalities. Each personality has its own patterns of behavior; the personalities may switch from one to another within a matter of a few hours. One evening a friend and I were counseling a young girl who took on twenty-five distinct personalities. One was very stubborn and acted like a little child, saying, "No, I'm not going to tell you!" Another was a jovial personality, laughing constantly. Still another was a personality who was bored with everything. Each of these personalities was an evil spirit that had a specific function in this girl's life in order to destroy and defeat her. If she had gone to a counselor who did not understand spiritual warfare, she would have been in a mental institution today. The interesting thing about this situation is that the girl was not aware of the demonic personalities while they were in control, but when we talked about each one of them she readily recognized them as voices and thoughts that were continually present in her mind.

*Let me re-emphasize that these symptoms by no means always show demonic activity.* They should not be taken in isolation; if there is a demonic problem other symptoms are normally present. *Remember, these are used only as indicators of possible demonization.*

## TESTING OF SPIRITS

This biblical injunction is found in I John 4:1, "Beloved, do not believe every spirit, but test the spirits to see whether they are from God; because many false prophets have gone out into the world." Dr. John R. W. Stott in his commentary *The Epistles of John* says about false teachers who are mouthpieces for evil spirits:

> Some of them claim some special revelation or inspiration to authenticate their particular doctrine. There is an urgent need for discernment among Christians. We are often too gullible, and exhibit a naive readiness to credit messages and teachings which purport to come from the spirit-world. There is such a thing, however, as a misguided charity and tolerance towards false doctrine. Unbelief (believe not every spirit) can be as much a mark of spiritual maturity as belief. We need to preserve the biblical balance, avoiding on the one hand the extreme superstition which believes everything and on the other extreme suspicion which believes nothing.[20]

Today there is much bewilderment about testing spirits. The purpose is not simply to distinguish evil spirits from "good" spirits—more than this is involved. This in itself is a trick of the devil, for we know that Satan sends out many "good" spirits. We must test to distinguish all spirits from the Holy Spirit. Four basic tests are given in the Bible to discern Satan's spirits, whether "good" or bad, from the Holy Spirit. The first three are specific tests meant to confront the spirits directly. The last is a more general test, but is still very significant.

The first test is based on this truth: "Every spirit that confesses that Jesus Christ has come in the flesh is from God" (I John 4:2). The Holy Spirit acknowledges the incarnation of the Lord Jesus—that he was a real man as well as being God.

The second test is from Paul's instructions to the Corinthians: "Therefore I make known to you, that no one speaking by the Spirit of God says, "Jesus is accursed"; and no one can say, "Jesus is Lord," except by the Holy Spirit" (I Corinthians 12:3). This is an acknowledgment of the Lordship of Jesus Christ. An evil spirit knows that Jesus is the Lord, but will never confess him as Lord. His lord is Satan! Satan encourages talk and activity about Jesus, but not about the Lord Jesus Christ. I become suspicious of groups who are always speaking of Jesus, but hardly ever speak of him as the Lord Jesus.

The third test is that the Holy Spirit will acknowledge the shed blood of the Lord Jesus that has power to cleanse from sin—the evil spirit will deny this (I John 5:6-7). We are told in I John 3:8 that Christ came "to destroy the works of the devil." He did this when he shed his blood on the cross (Colossians 2:15). That is why Revelation 12:11 proclaims that believers overcome Satan "by the blood of the Lamb." A devotee of Hare Krishna had been busy chanting when the blood of the Lord Jesus Christ was mentioned to him— he literally jumped up and ran in fear! This young man was the mouthpiece of an evil spirit; although he did not give us a chance to ask him, words were not necessary beyond his immediate reaction!

These three specific tests must confront the spirit directly. In other words, we are testing a spirit, not the person affected by a spirit. In many cases the spirit must be in operation in order to test it. An illustration of this was a woman who had "received the gift of speaking in tongues." She was challenged to test this spirit that spoke through her lips to see if her new gift was from God. To test the spirit by the three first methods was futile, because this woman acknowledged the incarnation, the Lordship, and the blood sacrifice of the Lord Jesus. But to actually test the spirit she had received was an altogether different issue. While she prayed in tongues, another prayed and tested the spirit that was operating through her at that moment. The spirit went into a rage and acknowledged that his lord was Satan!

Today, clear cases of demonic control are uncommon, that is, when a demon totally controls a person's faculties. Best described as an abrupt change in personality, in this condition someone's whole appearance becomes altered, possibly by facial grimaces, bodily contortions, a strange and glassy-eyed stare, half-shut eyes, a change in voice or different moods. The first three tests of spirits apply to this kind of situation. In order to gain spiritual freedom, a believer should immediately begin to pray out loud for the person oppressed, thanking the Lord for the victory that can come through the blood of the Lord Jesus Christ. The believer should use the three tests above to question the demonic spirit that controls the personality. If there is verbal opposition or a violent physical reaction to the tests from this strange demonic personality, the believer should command it to come out of the person oppressed in the name or by the shed blood of the Lord Jesus Christ. I would advise another believer to be present during this time because these reactions are sometimes quite violent. It is normal to need to repeatedly command the evil spirit to come out, as Jesus had to do in Mark 5:8. If there is no opposition to the three tests, the believer should pray together with the one oppressed to resist any possible demonic activity or deception.

The fourth test is that the Holy Spirit acknowledges *only* what is biblical, while an evil spirit moves in two directions—toward extra-biblical and non-biblical activity. Extra-biblical experiences and teachings "go beyond that which is written" (I Cor. 4:6). An illustration of this is the slaying of the Spirit that we spoke about as part of the religious trap. The Bible warns against accepting experiences, as if from God, that are not mentioned in his Word.

The non-biblical experience involves the misuse of biblical teaching through its misinterpretation, misapplication, and overemphasis. Satan creates much deception and confusion this way, especially in the charismatic movement and through the experience of speaking in tongues. I am convinced that most of the tongues-speaking experience in the mainstream of the charismatic movement does not represent a valid, biblical experience. I do believe that God may give the gift of speaking in tongues to believers today. Although I am not saying I believe the charismatic movement is of the devil, Satan is having a heyday deceiving people through the misinterpretation, misapplication, and overemphasis of this biblical experience.

There seems to be a misinterpretation of the biblical purpose for speaking in tongues that has been explicitly stated in I Corinthians 14:22: "So then tongues are for a sign, not to those who believe, but to unbelievers . . . . " Personal edification is an accompanying result, as it is with the exercise of any spiritual gift. Praying to, praising, or singing to the Lord in tongues is not mentioned in the Bible.

There is also a misapplication of ways to exercise tongues prevalent in many Christian groups today. Paul gives five guidelines for speaking in tongues in a group of believers. They are: (1) it must be a language (I Corinthians 14:11), (2) two or three at the most are to speak at any given meeting (I Corinthians 14:27), (3) each is to speak in turn and not at the same time (I Corinthians 14:27), (4) there must be an interpreter (I Corinthians 14:27-28) and (5) women are not to speak in tongues in the assembly (I Corinthians 14:34).

Finally, many overemphasize speaking in tongues. People urge others to have this wonderful experience—some claim it will change your life, give you more power, or allow you to move into the fullness of the Christian life. It is difficult to understand this emphasis when the Bible certainly does not say that a person needs this experience to move on to any new spiritual depths. Paul wrote eighty-six chapters, mentioning tongues in only three, and there only to straighten out the misuse of this gift. It is not mentioned in the Gospels or the Epistles, except for I Corinthians. The entire book of Colossians, that teaches about a believer's fulness in the Lord, does not mention the gift of tongues. And not all believers should speak in tongues (I Corinthians 12:30). We are never commanded in Scripture to speak in tongues. Many times charismatic meetings overemphasize the Holy Spirit. The Lord Jesus said that the Holy Spirit will not speak of himself, but will constantly glorify the Lord Jesus Christ (John 16:13-14). We have a tendency to overemphasize our feelings and experiences. This can turn us around to living by sight rather than living by faith. This is a very vulnerable position on which to stand in our experience-oriented culture—especially with Satan's readiness to deceive us.

Another overemphasis is in the area of the miraculous. There seems to be an assumption today that God will manifest himself through showy miracles. In order to back this up, some repeat the slogan: God is the same yesterday, today, and forever. This implies that God normally deals with man through spectacular events and miracles. The contrary is true! The Lord has revealed himself through the spectacular and miraculous only a total of 125 to 150 years in all of history. These years include the special work of God through Moses and Aaron, Elijah and Elisha, and Jesus and his apostles. Therefore, if God does express himself through the miraculous, it will be the exception rather than the rule.

Whatever the result of misinterpretation, misapplication, or overemphasis of any biblical truth, Satan is delighted with it. Believers must be careful not to get off on a tangent, centering their lives on other things than on Christ himself. The main purpose of the Christian life is to become like the

Lord Jesus. It is extremely important that believers diligently move toward Christlikeness and spiritual maturity.

Testing spirits involves spiritual discernment, and this comes only from God's Word. Paul says that "he who is spiritual (mature) appraises all things" . . . (I Corinthians 2:15, parentheses added). A young believer cannot be expected to discern all things, therefore he should be extremely cautious.

To sum up our discussion in this chapter, here are four steps to detect the activity of demons. *First, consider the possibility of any physical problems.* This may necessitate a thorough physical examination. I had one recent case of a young man who previously had had demonic activity in his life and had come back with more problems. An immediate conclusion would be that these problems were more of the same, but through careful examination it was obvious that he needed a complete physical. The doctor found a problem that warranted attention, and now with a special diet this man's problem has been alleviated. It is so important to check out any possibility of a medical problem.

*Second, search out violations of biblical principles.* Many problems stem from not following the clear principles of life laid out in the Bible, either from ignorance or disobedience. This is an important step before considering possible demonic activity. A Christian can never truly say "the devil made me do it." The believer always chooses to sin, thus opening the door for Satan to do his work. Through violation of a biblical principle Satan begins to harass the believer and can possibly progress in his attack to influence or control. Search out, list, and confess violations of God's Word!

*Third, discern any form of demonization under symptoms of attack.* List any symptoms that seem to clearly indicate a pattern of demonic activity. Pray for spiritual perception as you probe.

*Fourth, test the spirits.* Note where there are clear differences with the Holy Spirit's working and make the four tests explained from God's Word. It should be obvious through these steps what possible areas in a person's life are open to demonization. Now he or she is ready to learn how to fight Satan on all three battle fronts.

# CHAPTER 2

# Reckoning

To fight the spiritual war triumphantly, we must face all three battle fronts—the flesh, the world, and Satan. In these last three chapters each front will be considered, presenting biblical principles for victory.

Paul writes the most complete passage in the Bible on spiritual warfare in Ephesians 6:10-18. A strategy for each front is explicitly presented. The first verse of this section tells us how to fight the spiritual war against the flesh: "Finally, be strong in the Lord, and in the strength of His might" (Ephesians 6:10). Paul says this kind of battle requires strength from the Lord. At first glance this statement seems rather trite, but in his brief comment from Ephesians Paul has said a mouthful. If a person can grasp what Paul refers to here, his or her spiritual life will be significantly affected.

"Be strong in the Lord" means to be made strong in our union with the Lord Jesus Christ; it is this union that is the source of the believer's power. What does it mean to be in union with the Lord? No doubt what Paul had in mind was what had happened at Calvary. It was at Calvary that the Lord Jesus destroyed the basis of Satan's accusations. Satan has no basis for accusing believers who have trusted in Christ's death on the cross. The sin basis for Satan's accusations was nailed to the cross with Jesus:

And when you were dead in your transgressions and the uncircumcision of your flesh, He made you alive together with Him, having forgiven us all our transgressions, *having cancelled out the certificate of debt consisting of decrees against us and which was hostile to us; and He has taken it out of the way, having nailed it to the cross.* When He had disarmed the rulers and authorities, He made a public display of them, having triumphed over them through Him. (Colossians 2:13-15, italics added)

It was also at Calvary that the Lord Jesus destroyed the power of death:

Since then the children share in flesh and blood, He himself likewise also partook of the same, that through death He might render powerless him who had the power of death, that is, the devil; and might deliver those who through fear of death were subject to slavery all their lives. (Hebrews 2:14-15)

The battle was won at the cross. We are victors through Christ. We are not to fight for victory over Satan and his demons, we can stand as a victor. There are still a few battles to fight, but the war is over—we have won in Christ!

It was at the cross that God "delivered us from the domain of darkness, and transferred us to the kingdom of His beloved Son, in whom we have redemption, the forgiveness of sins" (Colossians 1:13-14). Whereas before our position was in the "domain of darkness," now we have been transferred into a new position—in Jesus Christ. We were once in Satan's domain, but now we are in Christ. The phrases, in Christ, or in Him, are used 164 times in the New Testament by Paul to give us an important concept for our daily lives as believers in the Lord Jesus Christ. The baptism of the Holy Spirit is the ministry of God whereby He places the believer in Christ. This happens at the time of conversion and thus is true of all believers (I Corinthians 12:12-13). Through this baptism we are identified with the body of Christ—we are in Christ.

God views all believers in this eternal position, no matter what their present experience might be. The following five gifts are ours: (1) In Christ "we have redemption, the forgiveness of sins" (Colossians 1:14), (2) we are made righteous in Him as, "He made Him who knew no sin to be sin on our behalf, that we might become the righteousness of God *in Him*" (II Corinthians 5:21, italics added), (3) we are complete in Him as Paul states, *"in Him* you have been made complete . . ." (Colossians 2:10, (4) he "blessed us with every spiritual blessing in the heavenly places *in Christ"* (Ephesians 1:3, italics added) and (5) in him we are also "sealed for the day of redemption" (Ephesians 4:30). This sealing is the security of the believer, who knows that God will preserve his own until the day that Jesus returns.

It is because of this new position in Christ that Paul addresses even worldly Corinthians as saints and holy ones. It is in this position in Christ that we are freed from the power of sin (Romans 6:7). Positional truth is true about us, regardless of how we feel. It is truth based upon revelation given in the Word of God concerning all believers. Every aspect of positional truth is shocking, because in practical day-to-day experience things do not seem to reflect our position in Christ. The question is, "How can I live like that in my experience?" The Lord has made a way for us to do just that, as he has made a new creation within us: "Therefore if any man is *in Christ,* he is *a new creation*: The old things passed away; behold, new things have come" (II Corinthians 5:17, italics added). This "new creation" is our new creature. God has performed a significant spiritual operation, and here is how it happened.

As we have seen, an unbeliever is totally under the control of the flesh or his sinful nature. His will is enslaved to the flesh, so that he can only function through his capacity to sin. This interlocking relationship between the will and the sin nature, (flesh) is called the old man.

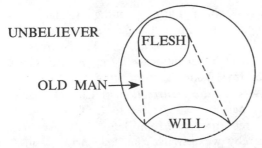

UNBELIEVER

OLD MAN

We learn in Romans 6 that we have died with Christ. Since we are dead in him, we are legally freed from the obligation to obey sin (Romans 6:7). "Death pays all debts, so the man who has died with Christ has his slate wiped clean, and is ready to begin his new life with Christ freed from the entail of the past." [21] Romans 6:6 clearly presents what happened in this death: "knowing this, that our old man was crucified with Him, that our body of sin (flesh) might be made powerless that we should no longer be slaves to sin." [22]

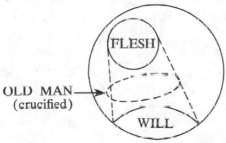

OLD MAN
(crucified)

The interlocking relationship between the will and the flesh, or the old man, was crucified. While the old man was destroyed, the flesh was not, it was simply "made powerless" over the will. In other words, the will is no longer enslaved to the flesh to do sinful works, although it may still yield to the lusts of the flesh at any time. Through union with Christ's death we have been set free from the control of the flesh—the power of sin.

Paul continues his explanation by pointing out that "if we have become united with Him in the likeness of His death, certainly we shall be also in the likeness of His resurrection" (Romans 6:5). Through our union with the *death* of Christ we have been set free from the control of the flesh, and through our union with the *resurrection* of Christ we have been given a new nature that is alive to God. This is the new creation, our reborn spirit (John 3:6-7). It gives us a new capacity whereby we can live the "in Christ" kind of life in our daily experience. The interlocking relationship between the will and the newnature, our reborn spirit, is called the "new man" (Colossians 3:10; Ephesians 4:24, KJV).

BELIEVER:

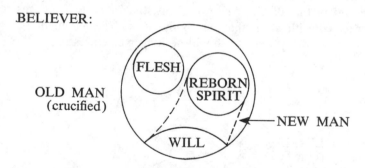

OLD MAN
(crucified)

FLESH

REBORN SPIRIT

WILL

NEW MAN

Now as believers we have a choice—we can walk (exercise our will) by means of the spirit, in our new nature, or walk (exercise the will) by means of the flesh, our sin nature, (Galatians 5:16).

You may say, "That's all well and good that I now have a new creation in me so that I can live the "in Christ" life; but practically speaking how do I operate through my new nature without giving in to the lusts of my flesh?" Paul answers this in verses 8-11 of Romans 6:

> Now if we have died with Christ, we believe that we shall also live with Him, knowing that Christ, having been raised from the dead, is never to die again; death no longer is master over Him. For the death that He died, He died to sin, once for all; but the life that He lives, He lives to God. *Even so consider* (*reckon*) *yourselves to be dead to sin, but alive to God in Christ Jesus.* (parentheses and italics added)

Since we have died with Christ, and have been raised from the dead with Him, we are to reckon ourselves "to be dead to sin, but alive to God." Reckon, the second command in the book of Romans, means to count on something as true, or to adopt a mental attitude believing that it is true. Here believers are commanded to adopt a mental attitude, believing that they are freed from sin's power through death and are now alive to God. This is to be counted as true regardless of what your feelings relate to you. It is true, however, not because of our reckoning on it, but because it is a fact revealed by God. Dr. F. F. Bruce notes:

> This 'reckoning' is no vain exercise but one which is morally fruitful, because the Holy Spirit has come to make effective in believers what Christ has done for them, and to enable them to become in daily experience, as far as may be in the present conditions of morality, what they already are 'in Christ'. . . .[23]

In the popular book *Psycho-Cybernetics,* Dr. Maltz, a plastic surgeon, tells in the introduction how he got involved in self-image psychology. The thing that started him thinking was an experience with a duchess who had had a tremendous hump on her nose. She had come to him for plastic surgery and afterwards enjoyed a classic nose and face that was truly beautiful. However, even though the facts were now different, she continued to play the part of an ugly duckling, an unwanted sister. Comparisons of photographs, before and after, were to no avail. Friends and family who could hardly recognize her raved over her new beauty. Still she denied any change had been made. By some strange mental alchemy she would rationalize that, although she could see that the hump was no longer on her nose, her nose still looked the same! She refused to reckon on the facts revealed from her mirror and consequently was miserable.[24]

Believers do the same as the duchess! God has removed us from the power of sin, and yet we look on ourselves under its power. God has created a new capacity by the Holy Spirit through which we are alive toward Him, and yet we act as if that capacity does not exist. We look in the mirror of God's Word and see ourselves dead to sin and alive to God—and live like nothing ever happened to us because of Christ's death and resurrection! We are to reckon or count it as true, which is not just a simple belief in something, but means to be *convinced* of it. When someone is convinced of a matter, he acts on it. We are to reckon in this manner concerning two entities—the old nature (flesh) and the new nature.

Many believers stop in their spiritual experience at Romans 6:11, reckoning, and never proceed with the action steps Paul lays out so clearly in the next two verses. There is no reckoning without these action steps.

*Therefore do not let sin reign* in your mortal body that you should obey its lusts, and *do not go on presenting* the members of your body to sin as instruments of unrighteousness; but *present* yourselves to God as those alive from the dead, and your members as instruments of righteousness to God. (Romans 6:12-13, italics added)

There are two decisive steps that extend beyond reckoning. The first Paul gives in two imperatives—"do not let sin reign" and "do not go on presenting." These refer to our sin nature, the flesh. Since we are dead to the flesh, we should stop letting sin reign. "And do not go on presenting the members of your body to sin" explains specifically how someone "lets sin reign," by yielding his will to the flesh and obeying its desires. Paul simply tells us to stop obeying the flesh.

The second action step is "present yourselves to God." It is now possible to make such a presentation to God, because we have become alive from the dead. We are no longer spiritually dead toward God, but alive in our reborn spirit, our new nature. The main issue in both of these action steps is obedience. Paul says we must yield in order to obey God through the new nature.

It is interesting to note that both of these steps demand that the believer be responsible for acting. So much is being taught today that puts out of balance what man does and what God does in the daily Christian life. Some say that if a believer will yield himself to God, God will do the rest. Another way of saying the same thing is let go and let God. This certainly sounds good, but it actually is not biblical. God has done his main operation in our lives by bringing us into a union with the Lord in his death and resurrection, thus providing us freedom from the power of sin and new life toward God through our new nature. The creator and resident of that new nature is the Holy Spirit; we have the availability of his works of teaching, guiding, reminding, convicting, and encouraging in that new nature. There is no such thing as a mystical takeover (other than a temporary, sovereign anointing of the Holy Spirit for special tasks) where God lives the Christian life through us. He has enabled *us* to live the Christian life. Paul often has been misunderstood when he wrote:

> I have been crucified with Christ (therefore dead to sin); and it is no longer I who live, but *Christ lives in me* (not through me); and the life which *I now live* in the flesh *I live by faith* in the Son of God, who loved me, and delivered Himself up for me. (Galatians 2:20, parentheses and italics added)

The very fact that we have a new nature, with the resident ministries of the Holy Spirit, sums up our capacity. We are to reckon on what God has done in freeing us from the power of sin to enable us to live for him. Then we must act on the basis of that reckoning—we must stop obeying the flesh and yield in order to obey God through our new nature.

These two action steps are in perfect agreement with the emphasis of the rest of Scripture. In Ephesians 4:22-24 it is phrased more clearly. Paul says:

> . . . in reference to your former manner of life, you *lay aside the old self* (*old man*), which is being corrupted in accordance with the lusts of deceit, . . . and put on the *new self* (new man), which in the likeness of God has been created in righteousness and holiness of the truth. (italics and parentheses added)

Here it is—put off the old self and put on the new self! Again, this is an act of the believer. No one will do this for you—not even God. It boils down to obedience! This is not just a blind act of obedience; it is acting by faith, walking in him by faith (Colossians 2:6). Walking by faith is the balance. We trust 100 per cent, trusting that God will give 100 per cent. We do all that we can do, walking by faith, and God does all he can do. The great missionary William Carey expressed the balance when he made the now popular statement, "*Attempt* great things for God, and *expect* great things from God." "Attempting" is what we do; "expecting" is what we trust God to do. Someone else has said, "We do the possible and God will do the impossible."

The believer has all of the enablement his new nature needs to live the Christian life, now he must commit himself to do it. Linked very closely with the issue of obedience is discipline. Most Christians are so far from the mark in the areas of obedience and discipline that when these terms are even suggested, the natural tendency is to protest against legalism! The Bible is opposed to legalism, but not to obedience and discipline. It is through proper discipline that godliness comes: . . . "discipline yourself for the purpose of godliness; for bodily discipline is only little profit, but godliness (discipline) is profitable for all things, since it holds promise for the present life and also for the life to come" (I Timothy 4:7b-8, parentheses added). It takes real discipline to put off the old man with all of the old sinful habits and to put on the new man with all of the new habits of holiness.

How then are we to fight the spiritual warfare on the battlefront of the flesh? The answer is twofold: (1) we must reckon ourselves to be dead to sin, the flesh, through our union with the death of Christ, in order to put off the old man. (2) We must reckon ourselves to be alive to God, in our new nature or reborn spirit through our union with the resurrection of Christ, so that we can put on the new man. This is what is behind the command of Ephesians 6:10. "Be strong in the Lord." In a battle such as this we must get our strength and power from our union with the Lord in his death and resurrection. In this union alone is there freedom from the power of the flesh and strength to live in the reborn spirit. *Reckon on it!*

# CHAPTER 3

# Renewing

We have dealt with the battle front of the flesh where Satan attacks on the inside; now we must move to the battle front of the world where Satan attacks on the outside. The world system is a vast front, with its pleasures, enticements, and values opposed to God. From the moment of birth, we are continually being programmed by principles of this world system that teach us how to live for ourselves without God. Believers are so saturated with those principles that Satan has an easy time on this battle front, without a doubt the most neglected of the three.

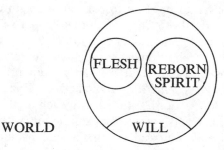

The only possible way to fight spiritual warfare on this front is through reprogramming the mind. After we have reckoned ourselves dead to the flesh and alive to God, and have made the proper commitment to obey God through our new nature, we are commanded not to fit into the mold of this world, but to be totally changed inside out by a process of renewing our minds. Paul put it this way: "And do not be conformed to this world, but be transformed by the renewing of your mind . . . " (Romans 12:2). In Colossians 3:10 Paul speaks of the new man being renewed to a true knowledge of Jesus Christ. This passage tells us how to combat the principles of the world system that oppose God —we must reprogram our minds according to God's eternal principles! In a Christless world this makes us more Christ like.

Renewing the mind does not so much involve you getting into the Word—though this is necessary—it involves getting the Word into you! The Bible is saturated with promises about meditation, allowing the Word of God to abide in you. There is a valid connection between meditation and overcoming Satan:

> I have written to you, fathers, because you know Him who has been from the beginning. I am writing to you, young man, because you are strong, and the *word of God abides in you,* and you have overcome *the evil one.* (I John 2:14, italics added)

In Ephesians Paul prepares the believer to resist Satan "in the evil day" (Ephesians 6:13). This refers to the day Satan decides to attack him particularly. The main preparation for "the evil day", however, is to put on the spiritual "armor of God" (Ephesians 6:11). Each piece of this armor comes from the indwelling Word of God, giving us strength to fight the battle on the world front.

There are six items that Paul lists as the "full armor of God" (Ephesians 6:11). These are all necessary "that you may be able to stand firm against the schemes of the devil" (Ephesians 6:11). We desperately need the "full armor of God," "for our struggle is not against flesh and blood, but against the rulers, against the powers, against the world-forces of this darkness, against the spiritual forces of wickedness in the heavenly places" (Ephesians 6:12).

Paul is not bound to the lifestyle of a soldier; he is bound to presenting the truth. He likens the qualities needed for spiritual warfare to the physical characteristics of a soldier's armor. These six pieces of armor are: truth, righteousness, preparation of the gospel of peace, faith, salvation, and the Word of God. The first three, when related to the soldier's work, are translated as: having girded himself with truth, having clothed himself with the breastplate of righteousness, having shod himself with the preparation of the gospel of peace. They describe his act of fastening a piece of armor to the body. The last three are ones that the soldier must take up: the shield of faith, the helmet of salvation, and the sword of the Spirit. Each piece of armor will be explained.

" . . . having girded your loins with truth . . . " (Ephesians 6:14).

The soldier's belt was not just an ornament, but was very vital because it held the other pieces of armor in place. *Truth,* as a quality of life opposed to falsehood and lying, is essential to the warfare against the father of lies. We must gird ourselves with the belt of truth that holds all of the other pieces of God's armor together. This truth is the total content of the Word of God. ". . . *having put on the breastplate of righteousness . . .*" (*Ephesians* 6:14).

> The breastplate consisted of two parts: the breastplate, made of hard leather, bronze, or iron, and a corresponding plate covering the back. They were connected by leather straps or metal bands passing over the shoulders and fastened in front, and by hinges on the right side.[25]

*Righteousness* is to be put on as a breastplate. This righteousness is simply obedience to the Word of God.

" . . . *having shod your feet with the preparation of the gospel of peace . . .*" (*Ephesians* 6:15).

The function of the sandals is to ensure firm-footedness. Preparation, or readiness, seems to be the central point of this piece of armor. Because of the nature of our warfare, we must be mobilized for any attack. This means being able to use the Word of God—and knowing what it says. This facility enables a person to have firm footing and, therefore, *peace*—even in the heat of the battle.

" . . . *the shield of faith* . . . " (*Ephesians* 6:16).

The shield consisted of two layers of wood glued together and covered first with linen and then with hide: it was bound with iron above and below, and had an iron boss affixed to it.[26]

*Faith* has an interesting connection in I John 5:4:

For whatever is born of God overcomes the world; and this is the victory that has overcome the world—our faith.

This shield of faith comes from trusting in, relying upon, believing, and counting on the Word of God. This shield will enable you "to extinguish all the flaming missiles of the evil one" (Ephesians 6:16b).

" . . . *the helmet of salvation* . . . " (*Ephesians* 6:17).

*Salvation* is the theme of the Word of God. It is the basis of our security; it is because of our salvation that we are able to fight in the first place. "This is our present salvation. That which saves and keeps safe and protects the head from a fatal or a disabling blow." [27]

" . . . *the sword of the Spirit which is the word of God*" (*Ephesians* 6:17).

This sword is likened to the short one used by the Roman soldier. It is the *Word of God*. The Greek term for word means the utterance of God, not the written Scripture, although it could be the written Scripture spoken. This sword is used by the Holy Spirit as an offensive weapon against Satan. An illustration of this is in Luke 4 when Christ was being tempted by Satan in the wilderness. The same Greek word is used to describe the offensive weapon the Lord used on Satan—He quoted scripture to him.

We must "put on the full armor of God" before resisting Satan. The best way to put on this armor is to allow the Word of God to abide in us. In other words, putting on this armor is the same as renewing our minds, or meditating. By putting on this armor we are fighting the battle front of the world.

The promises concerning renewing the mind are exciting! Here are some from different places in the Bible:

Joshua 1:8—Prosperity and success!
Psalm 1:2-3—Fruitful and prosperous!
Psalm 119:9, 11—Keeps from sin!
Psalm 119:97, 100—Wiser than all your teachers!
John 15:7—Answered prayer!
I John 2:14—Overcome Satan!

The process of renewing the mind takes time. I do not know of anything that is more profitable and life changing. Here is a way to do it.

Step No. 1 is intensive observation. Select a passage, at least a paragraph, that speaks to a problem or concern you are having. Go over, preferably memorizing, the passage until you really know it—feed your mind on God's principles in it! Most people start and stop right here—and therefore get very little benefit. This is like picking up a few pieces of armor, examining them, but neglecting to put them on for battle.

Step No. 2 is honest evaluation. Make a list of areas of weakness where you do not match up to the selected passage. For example, in I Corinthians 13 it says love is not jealous. Ask yourself, "Am I jealous?" If you are, then write it out—"I am jealous!" Be honest and specific! In this you are listing how you want to grow to be like the Lord Jesus.

Step No. 3 is thorough personalization. Run the passage through your mind over and over. Then pray, "Lord, whatever you have to do, work this quality into my life because I want to be more like you." That is a dangerous thing to pray unless you really mean it! The Lord is always looking for a believer whose heart is open to being changed into qualities of Christlikeness. He seems to send an angel "air mail special delivery" when we express that kind of attitude. In this step you must seek to apply the passage. Look for promises to claim, commands to obey, or sins to confess. Ask yourself the question, "What does this passage tell me to do?"

This process is just a suggested way to renew your mind. Use it, adapt it, or throw it out, but whatever you do RE-NEW YOUR MIND! There is no better way to become more like the Living Word, Christ, than to renew your mind through his Word. And there is no better way to put on the armor of God than by renewing your mind. It is in this way that you will be transformed, and will not fit into the mold of the world.

Renewing is the believer's action on the battle front that is the world. No wonder Satan wipes out so many believers —they will not take the time to renew their minds, and Satan catches them without their armor on!

# CHAPTER 4

# Resisting

Resisting Satan is the believer's action on the third battle front. On this front Satan and his demonic forces make direct attacks, usually after trapping a person by way of one of the other two battle fronts. Resisting Satan is one of the most neglected doctrines in Christianity today, yet it is the most common New Testament teaching on how to fight Satan, emphasized in the writing of Paul, Peter, and James.

Resisting is not the same as casting out demons. It is interesting to note that casting out demons is reported throughout the Gospels, but is not mentioned in the Epistles. In the Epistles we are taught to personally resist Satan. This is not to deny casting out of demons today: certainly there are cases in which Satan's control is so great that demons must be cast out. However, to cast out demons whenever a demonic problem is suspected is unwise and can be dangerous to someone's spiritual health.

There are many cases I have observed where casting out demons has been practiced irresponsibly. Two problems frequently occur. The first is the problem of re-entry. Casting out a demon leaves a vacuum in the person's life. The vacuum must be filled with something to block the demon's return. The only way to block that return is by meditating on a section of God's Word that deals with the particular sin that originally opened the door to the demon.

The second problem is the most common. It is the faulty diagnosis of demonization. Many self-appointed exorcists recklessly diagnose everything as demonic. The real tragedy is to the person who has been pronounced demon-possessed from no clear evidence of demonic activity. Usually the diagnosis is followed by a long two or three hour session of trying to cast out demons. Aside from complete exhaustion and spiritual defeat, the "demon-possessed" person becomes threatened by the possibility of demons inside him. This is a perfect time for real demonic forces to move in and have a ball encouraging his or her deep anxiety and depression. This can lead to actual demonization.

Overwhelmingly, the teaching of the New Testament is that the believer must resist Satan. Therefore, believers should be taught how to do this, to enable each one to fight successfully the spiritual war so that he or she will not be forced into dependence on a neighborhood exorcist.

There is more to resisting Satan than telling him to "get lost in the name of Jesus." Resisting rests upon two pillars; without them resisting is futile. The first pillar is reckoning —and there is no resisting it! The term resist basically means to stand, to stand as victor, to stand invincibly, or to stand successfully. On what are we to stand? We are to stand on the victory won at the cross, for in that victory Christ "delivered us from the domain of darkness, and transferred us to the kingdom of His beloved Son" (Colossians 1:13). We must stand on our position in Christ, united with him in his death and resurrection. Since we are in Christ, and he has all authority in heaven and earth, we are in the only place of victory, standing "in the Lord and in the strength of His might" (Ephesians 6:10).

The nature of our spiritual armor is based on the truth that we stand as victors. Every piece of the armor of God is defensive, with the possible exception of the sword, because the victory has already been won and now we need simply to stand our ground. Satan has been defeated at the cross (Colossians 2:8-15) and made powerless (Hebrews 2:14-15)—he has no right in any area of the believer's life.

The believer needs to stand on what is his in Christ, not to attack but to stand as a victor.

Peter's teaching on resisting adds to the concept of standing. Remember that Peter had been sifted like wheat (Luke 22:31) and used by Satan to trap the Lord Jesus. Peter knew what could happen. With his experience behind him, he was certain to warn other believers of the devil's schemes. In his letter, I Peter, he wrote a verse that is the favorite of many believers: "Casting all your anxiety upon Him, because He cares for you" (I Peter 5:7). This is an outstanding truth to share in a short devotional, but most believers stop and relax here. Peter does not stop his thought at this point. He immediately takes believers out of the clouds, shouting a warning in verses 8 and 9:

> Be of sóber spirit, be on the alert. Your adversary, the devil, prowls about like a roaring lion, seeking someone to devour. But resist him, firm in your faith. . . .

Peter says we should be on the lookout because the enemy, Satan, is a fierce destroyer who is out to get believers. The Greek words used here by Peter are the same as those used by Paul in Ephesians 6, but Peter adds the phrase "firm in your faith" from the Greek word *stereoi,* meaning to be as solid as a rock:

> 'Stereoi' implies solidity in the very mass body of the thing itself; steadfastness, mere holding of a place. A rock is 'stereoi,' firm, solid; but a flexible weed with its tough roots resisting all efforts to pull it up, may be steadfast! [28]

This is certainly appropriate coming from Peter, whose name meant the "rock".

Unless we reckon on our position in Christ (dead to the flesh, but alive to God), we have nothing on which to stand. Without reckoning ourselves dead to the flesh, we will be back under the control of the flesh and its lusts, constantly opening the door to Satan's accusations. Without reckoning ourselves to be alive to God, we will never enjoy the confidence and security of experiencing our life in Christ and standing victoriously.

In Christ we have authority to resist Satan, for it is in Christ that all authority in heaven and earth lies. Without reckoning on our position in Christ there is no power available to us from his sacrificial death to overcome the devil (Revelation 12:11). We cannot resist without reckoning!

The second pillar that supports resisting is renewing. There is no resisting without renewing! In Ephesians Paul clearly tells us that we must put on armor to resist Satan:

> Put on the full armor of God, that you may be able to stand firm against the schemes of the devil. . . . Therefore take up the full armor of God, that you may be able to resist in the evil day, and having done everything, to stand firm. Stand firm therefore. . . . (Ephesians 6:11, 13, 14a)

He tells us to "take up the full armor of God, that you may be able to resist." "Having done everything" means to be finished putting on God's armor. The phrase "that you may be able to resist" tells us that without the armor of God, a believer does not have the power to resist. Without renewing the mind, putting on the armor of the Word of God, a believer does not have the power or ability to resist Satan. There is no resisting without renewing!

Resisting without reckoning and renewing is a farce— and Satan knows it! If only believers were convinced of this, how different the spiritual war would be. Instead of hearing Satan's ridiculing laughter at our futile resistance, we would be hearing the fleeing footsteps of a defeated foe. We have the promise that if we resist him properly, Satan must flee (James 4:7). This proper resistance includes reckoning—acting against the flesh, renewing—acting against the world, and then resisting—acting against Satan.

Suspecting any demonic activity in his life, or as he helps another, a believer should act on each battle front to find relief. The steps of approach are the following: (1) List all areas recognized to be open doors for Satan's attack. (2) Acknowledge these as sins against God (I John 1:9) and tools used by Satan. (3) Reckon on your position in Christ! (4) Renew your mind—especially in the areas of attack. (5) Resist Satan audibly in the name of, or by the blood of, the Lord Jesus Christ. On the basis of God's Word, Satan and his forces will flee!

Paul closes his account of spiritual warfare as he encourages believers to pray and to be on the alert!

> With all prayer and petition *pray at all times* in the Spirit, and with this in view, *being on the alert* with all perseverance and petition for all the saints. . . . (Ephesians 6:18, italics added)

We must have the right attitude toward this war. We should pray all the time for our brothers and sisters in Christ who are also fighting against Satan—we must have compassion and concern, looking out for one another in this battle. Peter gives us another command to be of sober spirit, adding to the seriousness of our warfare. We dare not have an attitude that passively ignores the warfare, or an attitude that is flippant as though we were playing a silly game! Every day someone is trapped by Satan. Until believers learn to fight spiritual battles these prisoners will not be set free. Spiritual POW's never have a nice day!

# FOOTNOTES

1. *Newsweek,* "The Cult of the Occult", 75:96 (April 13, 1970), p. 96.

2. Kurt E. Koch, *Christian Counseling and Occultism* (Grand Rapids, Michigan: Kregel Publications, 1972), p. 22.

3. Kurt E. Koch, *Occult Bondage and Deliverance* (Grand Rapids, Michigan: Kregel Publications, 1970), I, p. 15.

4. R. C. H. Lenski, *The Interpretation of the New Testament* (Columbus, Ohio: The Wartburg Press, 1960), I, p. 499.

5. Ibid.

6. Ibid. (italics added).

7. Merrill F. Unger, *Unger's Bible Dictionary* (Chicago: Moody Press, 1966), p. 420.

8. Merrill F. Unger, *Biblical Demonology* (Wheaton, Illinois: Scripture Press Publications, Inc., 1952), pp. 105-106.

9. Lenski, *Interpretation of the New Testament,* p. 307.

10. Koch, *Occult Bondage and Deliverance,* p. 54.

11. A. J. Russell, ed., *God Calling* (Old Tappan, New Jersey: Fleming H. Revell Co., 1972).

12. Donald Grey Barnhouse, *The Invisible War* (Grand Rapids, Michigan: Zondervan Publishing House, 1965), p. 180.

13. Charles Hodge, *A Commentary on the Epistle to the Ephesians* (New York: Robert Carter and Brothers, 1856), p. 98.

14. Ruth Paxton, *The Wealth, Walk, and Warfare of the Christian* (New York: Fleming H. Revell Co., 1939), p. 48.

15. R. C. H. Lenski, *Interpretation of the New Testament* (Columbus, Ohio: The Wartburg Press, 1960), VIII, p. 410.

16. Barnhouse, *The Invisible War,* p. 176.

17. Origen has suggested that Jesus' rebuke to Peter had the idea of 'come along and get in your rightful place behind me.' "Had our Lord meant that Peter was to resume his place as a disciple, He would have said 'Come' rather than 'Go' (Get behind me); and in urging anyone to follow Him He would not call him 'Satan.' " A. Plummer, *An Exegetical Commentary on the Gospel According to St. Matthew* (London: Robert Scott Roxburgh House, 1928), p. 233.

18. W. E. Vine, *Expository Dictionary of New Testament Words* (London: Oliphants Blundell House, 1969), p. 129.

19. A. T. Robertson, *Word Pictures in the New Testament* (Nashville, Tenn.: Broadman Press, 1943), II, p. 136.

20. John R. W. Stott, *The Epistle of John* (Grand Rapids, Michigan: Wm. B. Eerdman's Publishing Co., 1969), p. 153.

21. F. F. Bruce, *The Epistle of Paul to the Romans* (Grand Rapids, Michigan: Wm. B. Eerdman's Publishing Co., 1966), p. 139.

22. Author's translation.

23. Bruce, *Epistle of Paul to the Romans,* p. 139.

24. Maxwell Maltz, *Psycho-Cybernetics* (Hollywood, California: Wilshire Book Company, 1960), p. 7.

25. Marvin Vincent, *Word Studies in the New Testament* (Grand Rapids, Michigan: Wm. B. Eerdman's Publishing Co., 1965), III, p. 408.

26. Armitage J. Robinson, *St. Paul's Epistle to the Ephesians* (London: Macmillan & Co., 1904), p. 215.

27. Lenski, *Interpretation of the New Testament,* VIII, p. 673.

28. Vincent, *Word Studies,* p. 670.